Joan Wicken

A Lifelong Collaboration with Mwalimu Nyerere

Aili Mari Tripp

MKUKI NA NYOTA
DAR – ES – SALAAM

PUBLISHED BY

Mkuki na Nyota Publishers Ltd
P. O. Box 4246
Dar es Salaam, Tanzania
www.mkukinanyota.com

© Aili Mari Tripp, 2023

ISBN 978-9987-753-85-7

You will also find featured authors interviews and news about other publisher/author events. Sign up for our e-newsletters for updates on new releases and other announcements.

Distributed worldwide outside Africa by African Books Collective.
www.africanbookscollective.com

CONTENTS

ACKNOWLEDGEMENTS

My deepest gratitude goes to those who read and commented on the manuscript and provided extensive comments and reflections. They include (in alphabetical order) Paul Bjerk, James Brennan, Steven Feierman, Andrew Ivaska, Harold Miller, Anna Mwansasu, Leander Schneider, Stephen Wicken, and Marcia Wright. I am especially indebted to Anna Mwansasu, Joan Wicken's assistant, for providing a lovely preface to the book. I also am enormously grateful to my mother, Marja-Liisa Swantz, for introducing me to Joan Wicken, first as a child starting in the early 1960s and then later on in life as an adult. Many thanks to my research assistants, Monica Komer and Valeriia Umanets. Finally, I owe my sincerest gratitude to Walter Bgoya and Tapiwa Muchechemera for publishing the manuscript with such enthusiasm.

ABOUT THE AUTHOR

Aili Mari Tripp is Vilas Research Professor of Political Science at the University of Wisconsin-Madison in the United States, where she teaches African politics and gender and politics. She lived in Tanzania from 1960 to 1974 and later carried out research in Tanzania, publishing among other works a book, Changing the Rules: The Politics of Liberalization and the Urban Informal Economy in Tanzania (University of California Press, 1997, 2021).

FOREWORD

I am pleased to have the opportunity to write the foreword for a book on Miss Joan Evelyn Wicken. She was a special figure in Julius Nyerere's political life as President of the United Republic of Tanzania and beyond. Miss Wicken took a leading role in establishing the Tanganyika African National Union (TANU) Kivukoni College in Dar es Salaam. After Tanganyika gained its independence, she became the righthand Personal Assistant to the President. I had the rare opportunity of working closely with Miss Wicken from 1985 after Mwalimu Nyerere retired from the presidency. Before that, we were colleagues when I started working at the State House in 1973 and much later after he left the presidency when I served in President Nyerere's Private Office as one of the personal secretaries.

People interested in learning about Mwalimu Julius Nyerere must have wondered why he chose to have Miss Joan Wicken, a British citizen, as his personal assistant and, as it turned out, for life!

Miss Joan Evelyn Wicken came to Tanganyika in 1959 at the invitation of Mwalimu Nyerere, who was the leader of the TANU political party. Miss Wicken (as she liked to be addressed) was sent by the British Labour Party to start an ideological college in the country, similar to the Labour Party's Ruskin College in England. Joan Wicken was, therefore, the founder of Kivukoni College in Dar es Salaam. She travelled extensively around the country, asking for donations from local people to get money for the work. She also took part in establishing the Tanganyika Education Trust Fund. She was the Secretary of the Fund.

In 1960, after Kivukoni College was established, Mwalimu Nyerere asked Miss Wicken to stay and become his Personal Assistant. She accepted. Her work was primarily drafting speeches, statements, and letters to heads of state for the President. She also covered and took notes of the President's interviews with visitors from outside the country. But Miss Wicken also ensured she would see Mwalimu Nyerere every evening after office hours to exchange views and ideas. This initiative helped her to be very efficient in preparing excellent presidential speeches.

In 1985, when Mwalimu Nyerere stepped down as president and went back to his home village Butiama, he again asked her to continue as his personal assistant. Miss Wicken accepted but asked to stay and work from Dar es Salaam because settling in Butiama would be difficult for her.

In 1987, Mwalimu Nyerere was appointed Chairman of the South Commission, following the decision by intellectuals and leaders from the South to set up the Commission. The main objective was to study the post-war experience of developing countries and suggest how to secure sustained progress in the South while urging developing nations to be self-reliant and use their own resources. He asked Miss Wicken to establish the South Commission Chairman's sub-office in Dar es Salaam. Its headquarters was in Geneva. It was at this point that he jokingly told Miss Wicken, "Now you are going to be my personal assistant for life!"

The secret behind Mwalimu Nyerere clinging onto Miss Wicken as his personal assistant for all those years was purely professional. Miss Wicken would always refer to Mwalimu Nyerere as "my boss." Mwalimu Nyerere liked people who had integrity and were honest and hardworking. Miss Wicken had all those qualities. He was also attracted to Miss Wicken because she was a staunch socialist like him.

Among co-workers and other government officials and politicians, Miss Wicken was known to be a no-nonsense personal assistant to the president! But, deep down, she had a soft spot of love and kindness. She was also very Tanzanian at heart. Unfortunately, despite spending almost half of her life in Tanzania, she didn't change her nationality to become Tanzanian. She remained a British citizen. Her life story is well-narrated in this book based on her interview with Professor Aili Mari Tripp.

Miss Joan Everlyn Wicken was born July 12, 1925. She went to college and earned degrees in Philosophy and Economics. She became secretary in the Commonwealth Department of the Labour Party office in London. Miss Wicken came to Tanganyika in 1959. In 1994 she went back to England due to ill health. Still, she continued to assist Mwalimu Nyerere in his work as Chairman of the South Centre – a follow-up mechanism of the South Commission.

After Mwalimu Nyerere passed on October 14, 1999, Joan Wicken retired from the South Centre. She continued living in Keighley, Yorkshire, with her longtime friends Mike and Maureen Yaffey. But she never stopped 'working' for Mwalimu Nyerere, though. She had several trunks full of shorthand notebooks with notes she took when working as

Mwalimu Nyerere's personal assistant. These notes date back from the independence of Tanzania. Miss Wicken always insisted that she had to finish transcribing those shorthand notes for future generations to learn about Mwalimu Nyerere. She stated in her will that the notes should be embargoed for 30 years after her death!

Paying tribute to Miss Wicken, Lionel Cliffe wrote an article in *The Guardian* entitled, "An unsung figure from the North who contributed to the struggle of developing countries." Indeed, she was an unsung figure who contributed a lot in helping Mwalimu Nyerere try to fulfil his dream of building a socialist Tanzania.

Miss Joan Evelyn Wicken died peacefully in her sleep on December 3, 2004, in a hospital ward in Keighley, where she was admitted with pneumonia. She was an atheist. May her noble soul rest in peace.

Anna Julia Chiduo-Mwansasu
Retired Personal Secretary, State House and Retired President's Office Butiama, South Commission/South Centre offices, Dar es Salaam and Geneva and the Mwalimu Nyerere Foundation, Dar es Salaam
Kivule, Dar es Salaam, June 2021

INTRODUCTION

Former Tanzania's Attorney General Roland Brown[1] called Joan Wicken the "mirror of Julius Nyerere's mind." Professor Cranford Pratt described her as "the power behind the throne." Saida Yayha-Othman said she was "a constant shadow behind Nyerere, and like a shadow, sometimes preceding the subject and projecting a considerable impression."[2] This interview provides the first in-depth window into Wicken's own account of her relationship with President Nyerere, the founding father of Tanzania. But it also provides a glimpse into the life of this intensely private person who had strong views and convictions. It shows how she was part of a group of socialist-minded foreigners who fiercely supported the nationalist cause of

---

[1] Roland Brown was a friend of Wicken's and former Tanzanian Attorney-General (1961–65).

[2] Saida Yahya-Othman. *Becoming Nationalist, (Book Two of Development as Rebellion: A Biography of Julius Nyerere,* by Issa G. Shivji, Saida Yahya-Othman, and Ng'wanza Kamata). Dar es Salaam, Tanzania: Mkuki na Nyota Publishers, 2020. p. 160.

Tanzania. They included the early parliamentarians like Barbro Johannsen (of Swedish descent), Lady Chesham (of American descent), and Derek Bryceson (of British descent), as well as academic advisors like Reginald Green and other academics who worked in higher education such as Cranford Pratt and Colin Leys. Joan disliked talking about herself, but this account provides a detailed description of her own life, thinking, and experiences in her own words.

Nyerere and Wicken were inseparable for more than 45 years. She was his alter ego. She crafted his English language speeches and books, generally the product of lengthy discussions and exchanges of drafts between them. As the interview shows, Wicken often wrote the first draft of a speech and then she and Nyerere would go back and forth on the speech until he was happy with it. According to Anna Mwansasu, her long-time colleague at the State House, sometimes he adopted her drafts without changing even a comma.[3]

---

[3] Yahya Othman, p. 171. Anna Mwansasu worked at the State House as Nyerere's Personal Secretary from 1973 to 1985. She started working in the President's private office around 1978. After 1985, when Nyerere ended his presidency, she was transferred to Butiama to be his Personal Secretary. That is when

Wicken was Nyerere's personal assistant when he was prime minister, president, party leader, and eventually, head of the South Commission. Their collaboration was so extensive, and their views were so similar that people often could not tell the difference.[4] In the interview, she says as much when she observes that "we were at one on" basic principles. Like her, she felt that he never compromised on basic principles. The interview pulls the veil back on this enigmatic woman who had a hand in shaping Nyerere's presidency, and one could say even Tanzania's history. Yet, paradoxically, she took no credit for anything other than "making Nyerere's life a little easier." She took pride in her role as protector of Nyerere's image, which she guarded fiercely. In the interview, she continued to protect his image even after he died.

I have known Joan since I was a child because she was a family friend. I grew up in Tanganyika/

she worked very closely with Joan Wicken. When Mwalimu became Chairman of South Commision she returned to Dar es Salaam and continued to work with Joan Wicken. In 1997 Nyerere sent her to Geneva to work in the South Center office.
[4] Yahya-Othman, p. 170.

Tanzania[5] (1960–1974) as the daughter of Dr. Marja-
Liisa Swantz, who came to Tanzania as a teacher in
1952, and the Rev. Lloyd Swantz, who worked with
the Lutheran World Federation. In the early years,
we visited Joan at her home in the Salvation Army
compound in Kurasini, Dar es Salaam, as we did not
live too far from her. Later, when we moved to Mbezi,
outside of Dar es Salaam, Joan visited our home from
time to time. She often came to see her dear friend,
Barbro Johansson, a Tanzanian-Swedish Member
of Parliament and former head of the Tabora Girls
Secondary School. Johansson owned our home and
frequently stayed with us when she was in town.[6] The

---

[5] Tanganyika was named Tanzania after it merged with Zanzibar
in 1964.

[6] Barbro Johansson (1912–2000) came to Tanganyika with the
Church of Sweden and taught at Kigarama Teachers' College.
She constructed a girls' middle school in Kashasha, Bukoba in
1949. She was elected a member of parliament for TANU in 1959
representing Mwanza. A Swede by birth, she held dual citizenship
after receiving her Tanzanian citizenship in 1962. Johansson
was appointed headmistress of Tabora Girls Secondary School
in 1965, served as an advisor to the Tanzanian ambassador in
Sweden and on the board of the Dar es Salaam University. She
was also a close friend of President Nyerere. She advocated for
the liberation movements in southern Africa. In 1968, she was
awarded an honorary doctorate by Gothenburg University. She

list of guests at an event held at our home on 13 July 1974, which she attended, gives some idea of her circle of friends. The 30 guests included the Ambassador of Sweden; the High Court Justice, Harold Pratt, and the Kashmiri judge Abdulla Mustafa and his wife, Sophia Mustafa, who had been one of the Indian Members of the first Legislative Council (1958–1965). She was a journalist during this time. Also in attendance at the 1974 event was one of the most famous Tanzanian artists, Elimu Njau. He attended along with his four children and his brother. Other attendees were our American neighbour and a close friend of Nyerere, Lady Chesham (an MP), and Leena Wallenius, a visiting Finnish journalist.[7]

I interviewed Joan in Tanzania in 1987 and again in 1994 while carrying out research for my book on the informal economy in Tanzania.[8] This publication is based mainly on an interview I had with her on March 3–4, 2000, in Keighley, England, after she had retired.

....

was also a strong advocate for adult education and served as head of the Adult Education Section in the Ministry of Education in Dar es Salaam.

[7] Marja-Liisa Swantz. 2004. *Aikani Afrikassa*. Helsinki: Ajatus.

[8] Tripp, Aili Mari *Changing the Rules: The Politics of Liberalization and the Urban Informal Economy in Tanzania*. Berkeley and Los Angeles: University of California Press. 1997. [Reprinted 2021]

My mother, Marja-Liisa Swantz (referred to as MLS in the interview), visited her almost a month later, on April 1, 2000, and asked some follow-up questions for me, which are incorporated into the interview. I also included in this introduction extensive excerpts from a handful of letters I acquired from the papers of Barbro Johansson after she died. I borrowed them from Johansson's family and photocopied them as they were about to be thrown away. I do not know if they were ever officially archived. The letters reflect the close friendship between the two women, their mutual admiration for each other, and their shared interest in Tanzania's welfare and its continued socialist orientation. I hope that these primary materials will contribute to further reflection on the role of Julius Nyerere in Tanzania's history and the early years after Tanzania became independent.

My book, *Changing the Rules*, is fairly critical of the Nyerere years and many of the policies Wicken defends in the interview. In my book, I describe how the urban dwellers I interviewed in 1987–1988 endured and survived severe economic hardships. Wicken stoutly defended egalitarianism and the poor in the face of the corruption of the wealthy. Based on this, I found her lack of understanding or appreciation of how Nyerere's policies hurt ordinary people and forced them into everyday acts of economic duplicity somewhat baffling. Even more puzzling was her insistence that people had to abide by some of the challenging economic restrictions placed on them while they were already living in dire straits. She felt that these hardships were primarily a product of global inequalities and externally imposed austerity measures. For me, these external factors were part of the problem, but key economic policies that created distortions in the economy (restrictions on internal and external trade, artificially low prices paid to peasants for crops, overvalued currencies, etc.) were also to blame.

Despite our different diagnoses of Tanzania's economic woes, it is hard not to have tremendous respect for the values and principles by which she lived and the goals for which she strived. Tanzania made many gains under Nyerere in promoting universal education, adult education and literacy, and access to health services. However, many of these early gains were offset by the economic crisis that befell the country in the 1980s and the harsh structural adjustment policies adopted to rectify the distortions created in the economy.

Brief Biography

Joan was born on July 12, 1925, on the outskirts of London. She was raised in Plumstead, London, by her father, a factory worker and a trade unionist. Her mother was ill during her formative years. She died when Joan was seven, and Joan and her sister were raised by her aunt and father. She was strongly influenced by his identification with the Labour Party. After finishing secondary school at 15, she worked as a clerk in a garage, where she learned shorthand, typing, and bookkeeping.

She visited Tanganyika at the invitation of Nyerere, who was then Chairman of the Tanganyika African National Union (TANU). At the time, he was touring the country and making a case for independence. Wicken first met Nyerere when she worked at the Commonwealth Office of the Labour Party in 1956. She travelled to Kenya, Ghana, Tanganyika, and the Federation of Rhodesia and Nyasaland between 1956 and 1957 on an Alice Horsman Travelling Fellowship. She found Tanganyika by far the most interesting of the countries she visited. Her experiences there left an indelible impression on her. She described her visit to Tanganyika in her 1958 report to Somerville College, Oxford[9]:

> Although I had not originally intended to spend any time in Tanganyika, the necessity to cross this territory encouraged me to spend a few days looking at the famous coffee co-operative system in the Kilimanjaro area, and then I decided also to take advantage of an invitation from a personal friend to spend a few days in Dar es Salaam and see something of a nationalist movement in its early stages. This was, as it turned out, one of the most interesting and exciting parts of the tour, and I feel also that this experience provided a key to the understanding of much in the way of political trends which had previously escaped me.

In the report, she also described her host, Nyerere, as an "extremely modest person, who was often embarrassed" by his popularity among ordinary people. She was there at a time when he was banned from public speaking. She witnessed him give a talk in Dar es Salaam to members of TANU only. Five hours before the talk was to take place, news of it had spread throughout the town. She wrote:

---

[9] Wicken, Joan E. 1958. "African Contrasts." Unpublished report of Alice Horsman Travelling Fellow, 1956–7. Bodleian Library of Commonwealth and African Studies at Rhodes House, Oxford University, Mss.Afr.s172b.

On the arrival of the speakers, every chair was filled; people were sitting on the floor between the rows, in every aisle and up to the speakers' table. Every window was filled with heads, and still, there were as many people outside who could find no place (p. 36).

Her report captured the enthusiasm with which people embraced Nyerere and the force for independence that he represented. She continued:

It is, of course, true that organisations like T.A.N.U. get their main organisational strength from the urban areas. But I later found that support for T.A.N.U. at any rate, was not confined to these regions. One day I went with Mr Nyerere and his party of Central Committee officers to a village about 50 miles from the capital. A mile away from our destination, we were met by a crowd of people running down the road towards us, waving green branches which they had torn from the roadside trees. They then insisted on pushing the car for the rest of the way, singing triumphal chants as they did so, and just about every person of the village was gathered in the central square as we arrived there.

Again, on the 600-mile journey I took with them to the south of the country, we were greeted at every important village by a turnout of people, and in the two towns where we stopped, our Land Rover was escorted through the streets by dancing crowds. It is impossible to describe the scene: at Iringa, the view we had was of people running by the side of the Land Rover carrying hurricane or pressure lamps, and in front of the vehicle, the headlights picked up the moving legs and pale feet of people dancing. The noise was of excited, happy people, of trilling women, of song and laughter, and when we stopped at our destination, the street was full of people, their dark faces shining in the lights they carried. There was no speech. The President stood on a raised step, had a light held to his face so that the people might see him clearly. Perhaps they did not understand everything that was going on, nor the implications of all the slogans they chanted, but that he was their leader, that they were supporting him, that no one could doubt. It was in these outlying areas, some of which the President had never before visited, that I realised the full meaning and importance of T.A.N.U. and the responsibility of its leader. It was impossible not to be affected by this evidence nor to be unaware of the possibilities — and dangers — implicit in it.

It was during this trip through Africa that Wicken also came to deeply appreciate firsthand the indignities that Africans experienced every day under colonial rule. She had been travelling with seven TANU members throughout the country. She commented on one of her experiences of colonial racism during the trip that profoundly disturbed her:

One further experience of this journey is relevant. On the second day, after travelling for seven hours through the largely uninhabited Tsetse-ridden country, we stopped for a meal at a very attractive roadhouse. The European managers of this "Chimala Hotel" [in the Mbeya region] said scornfully that there was an

African place down the road we could go to, adding to me after further questioning by my hosts, "I will give you some sandwiches." Even to write this reminds me of my humiliation and anger at the insult which was thrown, in the name of whiteness which perforce I shared, to seven men who had shared everything with me on the hard journey and constantly made special arrangements for my comfort. A realization of the possible political implications of such treatment of these particular people only came later because they so obviously feel completely at one with the mass of their compatriots. Only the next day when one of them left me at the door of the hotel where accommodation had been arranged for me and said, "We don't want a repetition of yesterday," did I fully appreciate that they too had felt the humiliation which had forced tears of frustration and anger down my face. (p. 37)

Later Wicken returned to Tanganyika in 1960 on behalf of the Tanganyika Education Trust to set up Kivukoni College, along the lines of Ruskin College in the UK for adults. Wicken toured the country to raise funds from ordinary citizens for the college. Although the Kivukoni College ceased to exist after 1993, many Tanzanians, who later became leaders of the country, had their beginnings at this College. As Wicken reflected later in an unpublished paper about the College:

I comfort myself with thoughts of the thousands of men and women who expanded their knowledge at Kivukoni between 1960 and 1993 and of the great contribution to public development that many of them made. And some day, I believe a group of Tanzanians will get together and create a new residential adult education institution at Kivukoni.

Even after setting up Kivukoni College, Wicken remained an ardent advocate of adult education, which was primarily supported by the Swedish Agency for International Development (SIDA) after 1965.[10] Adult education in Tanzania involved such institutions as the Institute of Adult Education, the National Correspondence Institution, a national literacy programme, the Folk Development Colleges, rural libraries, radio education programmes, rural newspapers and mobile cinemas.[11]

---

[10] Communication with Emerita Professor Marcia Wright, June 11, 2021.

[11] Philemon A. K. Mushi Source, "Origins and Development of Adult Education Innovations in Tanzania Author(s)." *International Review of Education*, 1991, Vol. 37, No. 3 (1991), pp. 351–363; Anders I.Johnsson, Kjell Nyström and Rolf Sundén, *Adult Education in Tanzania*, SIDA Education Division Documents No. 9, March 1983. https://publikationer.sida.se/cont entassets/75cb19caa5644cc1a2d1f6169eb00dde/adult-education-in-tanzania---a-review_3611.pdf Accessed June 13, 2021.

In 1960 she started working as a speechwriter and personal assistant to Julius Nyerere. She remained in this post throughout his years as Tanganyika's Chief Minister (1960–1961), Prime Minister (1961–1964) and President (1962–1964), Tanzania's President (1964–1985), Party Chairman of Tanganyika African National Union[12] (1960–1977), Party Chairman of Chama Cha Mapinduzi (1977–1990), and finally head of the South Commission (1987–1995) and its successor, the South Centre (1995–1999). Before Nyerere stepped down as Tanzania's president, he held an award ceremony to mark the Union Day Celebrations. At the award ceremony, he presented Wicken with a medal of the order of the United Republic of Tanzania.[13]

Wicken was initially hired by the British civil service in 1960 to help Nyerere prepare for independence. She also helped write the inaugural independence speech in which he thanked the Tanganyikan people for their

---

[12] TANU was formed in 1954."
[13] "Nyerere Awards Medals," *Daily News, April 27*, 1985. http://41.86.178.5:8080/xmlui/handle/123456789/9704

contributions in bringing about independence.[14] Her last major initiative was to assist Nyerere in establishing the South Commission. She visited 31 countries with him in less than six months to meet heads of state. Later she helped set up the Nyerere Foundation in Dar es Salaam.

She drafted Nyerere's policy statements and speeches in English, putting his ideas on paper. She describes how the speeches and books resulted from an intense collaboration between her and Nyerere. It is also worth noting that many of Tanzania's foundational documents and policies were first written in English and later translated into Swahili. Future linguists may wish to consider the impact this might have had on the formulation of some ideas. Although she denied influencing Tanzanian politics, she certainly had a hand in articulating it as part of the State House team. There was probably no one who knew Nyerere as a politician better than Wicken. Roland Brown, a friend of Wicken's and a

---

[14] Kamata, Ng'wanza *Becoming Nationalist*, (Book One of *Development as Rebellion: A Biography of Julius Nyerere*, by Issa G. Shivji, Saida Yahya-Othman, and Ng'wanza Kamata). Dar es Salaam, Tanzania: Mkuki na Nyota Publishers, 2020, p. 79.

former Tanzanian Attorney-General (1961–1965), said that in dealing with his correspondence, she had a marvellous ability to write things for him that sounded like him.[15] She also assisted with his English-language correspondence based on consultations with him but was able to provide just the right tone, which he greatly appreciated.

After 1994, she returned to the UK to live with friends and later moved into a care home in Keighley. She typed up her shorthand notes, which she requested should be archived and sealed at Rhodes House Bodleian Library for 30 years after her death.

Joan Wicken as a Person

I first came to know Joan in the early 1960s when my family lived in Kurasini, not far from the Salvation Army compound where she lived. I recall she had a small white Fiat 500 saloon car in which she moved around Dar es Salaam.[16] She lived in a tiny white

---

[15] http://www.tzaffairs.org/?p=228#more-228
[16] Before acquiring the Fiat she had a faded red 50 cc Vespa scooter.

cottage with thatched roof, and bougainvillaea crept up the walls outside. She would sometimes, on Sunday afternoons, entertain people for tea. I remember seeing piles of books on a small table next to her armchair, and books and papers were strewn all over the house. She smoked a lot and enjoyed her whiskey, which was probably her only indulgence given the frugal woman that she was. When I visited her in Keighley in 2000, she said she was forced to give up the whiskey and smoking in her later years for health reasons.

She was extremely humble in not seeking any special privileges or accommodations. She regarded this as a point of pride. Wicken had been offered a larger house with pleasant gardens, but she turned it down, preferring to remain in her small, modest residence. She never put on airs or expected to be treated differently than most ordinary Tanzanians. In the interview, she talks about how ashamed she was when she was given a "big" car to drive around the countryside to raise funds for Kivukoni College. Wicken shunned lavish displays of wealth and ministers in fancy cars because she felt it set a bad example for poor folk. This comes through in the interview when she describes the wedding of George

Kahama's daughter and John Rupia's son.[17] It seems that even as a child, she exhibited a frugal sensibility as she recounted how she added water to paint to stretch it so she could finish painting a staircase.

Lionel Cliffe, a British professor, describes her small house when he visited her during the mid-1980s: "Cold water was brought in black buckets. Light came from a kerosene lamp; she cooked on kerosene hot plates, made her own clothes on an old hand-sewing machine — and enjoyed quilting. Joan became a much-loved figure to the staff and the many disabled children who lived on the Salvation Army compound. She was always willing to volunteer her help."[18]

When she retired, she refused to accept a resettlement compensation of £50,000 to offset the expense of moving to the UK.[19] When I visited her, she lived in a retirement home in Keighley, a Bradford

---

[17] https://medium.com/activate-the-future/international-womens-day-is-always-a-good-time-to-reflect-on-those-women-who-have-had-an-impact-on-beadc4460e45
[18] https://www.theguardian.com/news/2004/dec/21/guardianobituaries
[19] Nakasula, Mwaka. In "Joan Wicken, Tanzanians learn that hard work is the only justification to live," *The Guardian*, January 18, 2005.

district town that has been voted as one of the top 10 worst places to live in England. Not surprisingly, she maintained her modest lifestyle with sparse belongings. I recall her using a single potholder while cooking, which seemed a little precarious. Her scoliosis had worsened, but she seemed every bit as feisty as she had been in her earlier years.

Not surprisingly, she adhered to a strict work ethic and code of conduct while at the State House in Tanzania, according to Anna Mwansasu. As Mwansasu told me: "Ever since I started working with Miss Wicken, I got on well with her, I think because I was hard working! She turned out to be a great friend."[20] Wicken did not tolerate office gossip, tardiness, and unnecessary talk on the phone. She sought to replace employees who were deemed lazy. Nevertheless, she had a good sense of humour and was sociable. She even gave up her travel allowances to be shared equally among other staff workers.

Manilal Devani, who was at one time Mayor of Dar es Salaam and a close friend of Joan's, described her similarly as one of the most industrious people he had ever encountered. He noted that "She was such a busy

---

[20] Communication June 17, 2021.

person that she preferred to prepare her lunchtime sandwiches a week in advance."[21] She baked her own bread for the sandwiches. Wicken refers to herself in the interview "as a donkey at work."

According to the head of the Nyerere Foundation, Joseph Butiku, she worked past midnight most nights, even though she started work at 9 a.m. She generally spent late afternoons at Nyerere's home in Msasani, talking to him from 5 pm to 6 pm, discussing the day's events and planning the upcoming schedule. She also travelled a lot with him.[22] In one communication with Barbro Johansson, written on a card (n.d.) with a drawing of Azania Front Lutheran Church, Wicken complained about the amount of travel:

> I travel too much … I am well — just tired. Especially of travelling! We went to 41 [sic] countries last year! This year will be less — but more speeches seem to be on the Agenda, so there's still masses to do. Of course, it's usually very interesting, but living out of a suitcase is very difficult when it is most of the time. And work piles up, so there can be no rest in between. But the Chairman is well. He did have a break at Christmas and a short one

---

[21] Nakasula, Mwaka. In "Joan Wicken, Tanzanians learn that hard work is the only justification to live," *The Guardian*, January 18, 2005.

[22] Yahya-Othman p. 104

> since. All at Butiama, of course. He enjoys that and is
> reluctant to leave it!

Yahya-Othman notes that the long hours she spent with Nyerere roiled his wife, Maria Nyerere, from time to time. Maria's frustration may have come from the fact that Nyerere did not treat his wife as an intellectual equal like he did Wicken, no doubt leading to tensions. It is unlikely that she suspected a romantic affair between the two of them, even though there were such rumours at the time.[23] Wicken steered clear of talking about these tensions in the interview and spoke only in positive terms about Maria Nyerere. She also appreciated her important role in singlehandedly raising the family with little support from Nyerere. Unlike most other first ladies, Maria Nyerere was not afforded any special privileges, nor were his children. According to Mwakikagile, Nyerere did not allow people to refer to her as a first lady but rather as Mrs Maria Nyerere.[24]

---

[23] James R. Brennan cites such rumours having been published in the newspaper *Ukweli* ('Truth'), 28 July 1968, cited in "Julius Rex: Nyerere through the Eyes of His Critics, 1953–2013," In *Remembering Julius Nyerere in Tanzania: History, Memory, Legacy*, Ed. Marie-Aude Fouéré. Africae, 2020.

[24] Mwakikagile, Godfrey, *Life in Tanganyika in the Fifties*. New Africa Press, 2009.

As much as Wicken admired Nyerere, they never had a romantic relationship. The love of her life was Tom Mboya, whom she met in England when he was studying industrial management. He was an independence activist, a founder of the Kenya African National Union, who later held numerous cabinet positions as minister of Justice and Constitutional Affairs, Labour and Economic Planning and Development. He was assassinated at the age of 38. She told me about her relationship with him, and it is alluded to in the interview, but I left his name out of the interview at her request. Anna Mwansasu, her colleague at the State House, revealed this relationship in the 2020 publication by Yahya-Othman, so there does not seem any point in hiding it any longer.[25]

Wicken and Nyerere: A Meeting of the Minds

What comes through in the interviews is Wicken's intelligence and self-awareness through her confident assertions and self-deprecating humour. She can

---

[25] Yahya-Othman p. 6.

be totally herself and very British, yet at the same time, at one with Nyerere's goals for Tanzania as an individual entrenched in the political establishment of Dar es Salaam. She provides many recreations of dialogues she had with Nyerere, making it easy to imagine the banter between them. It is clear they had many common running jokes.

It could be said that Wicken was one of the many foreigners who fell under the spell of what Kenyan political scientist Ali Mazrui called "Tanzaphilia." Nyerere had captured their imagination with his ideological commitment to self-reliance and egalitarianism and his strong moral posture regarding the poor. Mazrui writes about how "there was a certain gentleness in Tanganyika's 'struggle' for independence, which made it hardly a struggle at all. And it was fitting that Tanganyikans should have accepted the leadership of a gentle personality like Nyerere."[26] They were drawn to this most intellectual of all English-speaking heads of states in Africa, according to Mazrui.

---

[26] Ali Mazrui, "Tanzaphilia: A Diagnosis," *Transition*, No. 31 (Jun.–Jul., 1967) p. 21.

Wicken was drawn from the outset to Nyerere, whom she saw as both a philosopher and someone who could relate to ordinary people. She explicitly stated in the interview that when she first travelled to Tanganyika in 1956 and compared the country to the other countries she visited in Africa, "I liked Tanganyika, which was much more gentle." She compared Nyerere to Malawi's Hastings Banda, who was bitter and angrily roused crowds during his visit to Tanganyika in 1960. She much preferred Nyerere, who was "hot" against the colonialists but made the crowds laugh and persuaded them why they needed independence.

Wicken was a woman of many contradictions. On the one hand, she was very opinionated and self-assured in her beliefs, such as her unwavering support of socialism. She had a sharp tongue. On the other hand, she completely submerged her own need for recognition behind Nyerere's agenda. No doubt, this was partly a function of her role as a speech writer, but also of the fact that she was not Tanzanian, something of which she was acutely cognizant. There were lines she would not cross, and she was extremely sensitive to her positionality as an outsider. At one point, she says, "I used to get horrified at the way some people [foreigners] thought they had all the answers. I didn't ever feel that, but I would argue from my own background." I have no doubt that she spoke freely with Nyerere, all the while maintaining a deferential and hidden public persona. As a result, Nyerere trusted her implicitly.

She made a point of not drawing attention to herself, and in the interview, of not taking credit for virtually anything at all. I asked her what her contribution was, and her reply was, "I made Mwalimu's job a little bit easier on the margins. I was helpful to him more than anything else."[27] This came not so much from a sense of modesty but more from her desire to stay out of the limelight. Yet clearly, she had an impact on Nyerere. One finds her visible in many state photos but always in the background, often with her head poring over her notes. I found only one official photo where she was in the foreground, and that was when she met the Queen of England with Nyerere. Yet based on the interview, there is little doubt that she had a substantial impact on Nyerere's thinking, and his speeches and books were a product of their intellectual collaboration.

---

[27] President Nyerere was often called "Mwalimu," which was the Swahili word for "teacher," which is a term of respect.

She made many self-deprecating comments throughout the interview, downplaying her own importance, from references to her failures in French and math as a student, to her deficiencies in economics that came into full view in a public debate in England. She talks about how she was a difficult daughter to her father and how she was a terrible first secretary of the Africa Education Trust. Michael Harrington, the famous American democratic socialist writer and activist who visited Tanzania in the mid-1970s, also noted her same self-effacing traits, which contrasted sharply with her actual role in Tanzania's political life. He described her as "a British woman, simply dressed, without makeup, with a warm, friendly, appealing face. But she is not, as I first feared, a dour, humourless fanatic. She is self-depreciatory, quick to admit mistakes, with no pretence to omniscience.… She is, I hear on all sides, one of the most important people here" (Harrington 1977, 183).[28]

Wicken portrays herself as a worker bee. Her job was to see to it that things got done. In her correspondence with Barbro Johansson, she writes

---

[28] Michael Harrington, *The Vast Majority: A Journey to the World's Poor*. Simon & Schuster, 1977.

about how in April of 1986, she had just written ten speeches and had three more to do and one to edit in six days.[29]

She was not hired as an advisor, but with time she became more comfortable in her role and identified more strongly with Tanzania's future. She had strong opinions of her own, which she shared with Nyerere. She argued with former president Benjamin Mkapa about privatisation, backed Nyerere on his decision not to run again for president in 1985, and expressed her opinion of Ethiopia's former president Mariam Mengistu. Thus over time, she evolved into a more fully rounded person.

Although Wicken was obviously more than an assistant, it is curious to note that numerous African presidents of Nyerere's early post-independence generation had British assistants or secretaries. It is possible that this was because they were not seen as politically threatening. Nyerere had a British Secretary, Mrs Wilson, whom Wicken talks about in the interview. The President of Ghana, Kwame Nkrumah (1909–1972), also had a British private

---

[29] Personal correspondence, Joan Wicken to Barbro Johansson, April 20, 1986.

secretary, Erica Powell OBE (1921–2007). Powell also served as the private secretary of the President of Sierra Leone (1905–1988), Siaka Stevens.

Although close presidential relationships with foreigners might have been non-threatening, there was always the possibility that outsiders might be surreptitiously working for external interests. Yahya-Othman cites concerns that Wicken might have been used by the British to ease Nyerere's ties with the Soviet Union. This is highly unlikely given her allegiance to Nyerere and non-alignment. If anything, Nyerere used her to interpret British and American objectives, as is implied in the interview. She seemed to believe that her reporting on the foreign diplomats to him was a way of ensuring that he knew what she was up to and that she was not compromised in any way.

Wicken was a perfectionist and fastidious in her attention to detail. She worried about petty things (e.g., what time a letter arrived, how long the letter took in the post).[30] This must have become unbearable for her and surprising to her co-workers in the 1980s, as life became increasingly difficult for

---

[30] Yahya-Othman.

ordinary people due to the decline in the standard
of living that everyone experienced, the shortages of
daily necessities, and the lack of transportation. Civil
servants focused on their small enterprises and farms
at the expense of their jobs.[31] It also must have caused
some consternation among those who worked with
her when she expected things to run like clockwork
as in the past. She did everything by the book as a
matter of principle at a time when formal procedures
were more than a little challenging. I found it difficult
to reconcile her insistence that people abide by rules
with her insistence that she was for the ordinary
person and the poor. There seemed to be a disconnect
between her identification with the poor and her lack
of appreciation for the constraints in which they
found themselves as a result of Nyerere's policies.

She sometimes took her "small is beautiful"
approach to lengths that greatly frustrated
development practitioners. Joseph Stepanek met
her in 1987 when he started a four-year term as
the Representative and Mission Director of the US
Agency for Development (USAID) in Tanzania. In

---

[31] Tripp 1997.

an interview, he described his shock at her insistence
that Tanzania should not adopt and use computers:

> I heard a lot about her and thought that the least I could
> do was to go and say "Hello" to her. I had a marvellous
> time. She was as lovely to meet as anybody's favourite
> aunt until she opened her mouth. Then you got quite
> a blast about the glories of socialism and the dangers
> of capitalism. I said to myself: "Well, I've managed to
> step on all of the land mines," and I thought that I'd get
> onto a safe subject. So I started to talk about computers
> and their value in modernizing Tanzania. She said: "No
> way. Computers put people out of work, and, besides,
> Tanzania is about to be self-sufficient in typewriters."[32]

To understand Wicken, one had to understand
Nyerere and vice versa. Yahya-Othman astutely
notes that in her personal correspondence, she often
used the collective "we" to refer to her, Nyerere, and
the Tanzanian government combined. I noticed the
same pattern in her interview as well, where some
of the time she was talking about her and Nyerere

---

[32] Interview with Joseph F. Stepanek. The Association for
Diplomatic Studies and Training Foreign Affairs Oral History
Project. Foreign Assistance Series. Interviewed by: W. Haven
North Initial interview date: December 29, 1997. Library of
Congress. https://tile.loc.gov/storage-services/service/mss/
mfdip/2004/2004ste07/2004ste07.pdf

as "we," but other times she was clearly referring to the country or government of Tanzania as well. Her identity was so intertwined with that of Nyerere and Tanzania that even she could not separate them in her mind. When I interviewed her on March 4, 1994, I asked her about some of the failures of the overreach of the state in economic development. She responded: "Look, we didn't know any more than anyone else about what we were doing. Nobody did. We did what seemed right at the time. We did the best we could." She felt that the donors also should have taken some of the blame. She abhorred donor arrogance. At that time, I asked if Nyerere regretted anything. She said there was remorse over the environment. Nyerere had not done enough: "We did not understand the effects at the time. Now he is trying to rectify this through the South Commission." Here, as in many places in the 2000 interview, the "we" was this triad that Yahya-Othman describes.

Much of her personality comes through in her comments about what she valued in Nyerere. She respected him above all for his concern for the general welfare of the people and his desire to uplift the poor. Her insistence on egalitarianism came through in other encounters as well. She told

Michael Harrington that success in Tanzania meant increasing the level of medical care and education for the poorest. She believed that a socialist society could be built at a low economic level and that Tanzania did not need the wasteful, destructive standard of living of a capitalist society like the United States in order to create a just society. She rejected the idea of state encouragement of the most efficient capitalist enterprise for farmers and envisioned a more egalitarian approach that benefited all rural dwellers. Sharp income differentials deeply disturbed her.[33]

In this interview, Wicken highlights how Nyerere fought against tribalism. Not only did he develop policies and create institutions that reinforced national unity, but he set an example for others to emulate. He was particularly appalled by the rise of tribalism after President Ali Hassan Mwinyi took over and continued to fight against it. This comes through not only in the interview but also in Wicken's correspondence with Barbro Johansson. He not only eschewed tribalism in Tanzania but also in other African countries as well.

---

[33] Harrington, 1977, 184.

Wicken wrote to Barbro Johansson in 1998 about how Nyerere had left the initiative to stop the renewed fighting in the Democratic Republic of Congo to Mandela and the South Africans and sought a supporting role instead. Nyerere had opposed Laurent-Désiré Kabila[34] because he was fomenting tribalism:

> Mwalimu never knew Kabila before the successful rebellion against Mobutu[35]— despite the latter having been in Tanzania for most of his exile. But Mwalimu was very pleased with the fall of Mobutu — who is the only African leader he publicly attacked for corruption and exploitation of the people both during and after being President. It is true that he was not impressed by Kabila when he did meet him during the fighting against Mobutu, but for a long time, he hung on to hope that once in power, Kabila could be influenced by

---

[34] Laurent-Désiré Kabila was the third President of the Democratic Republic of the Congo from 1997 until his assassination in 2001. He led a takeover of the country in 1996–97 by the Alliance of Democratic Forces for the Liberation of Congo (ADFLC), with the help of Rwanda and Uganda, overthrowing President Mobutu Sese Seko. Kabila studied at the University of Dar es Salaam.

[35] Mobutu Sese Seko was President of the Democratc Republic of Congo from 1965 to 1971 and of the country, which was renamed Zaire, from 1971 to 1997.

other SADC[36] leaders towards serving the interests of the people he had taken responsibility. More recently, Mwalimu has become very hostile; he says that not only has Kabila failed to work with other opponents of Mobutu, but he has turned on tribal grounds against the very people who helped him to get his current position. There is apparently a DRC (Democratic Republic of the Congo) radio station pouring out the same kind of anti-Tutsi murderous propaganda as was put out before the Rwandese genocide: Kabila himself makes such speeches — and rather than trying to control the Rwanda Hutu militia, he seems to be facilitating their killing raids into Rwanda. And unfortunately, it seems that even within Tanzania, there are now people talking in such murderous tribal terms — including people within CCM! … Mwalimu is attacking the racism/tribalism which is growing up in Tanzania — and which most of the private press is supporting.[37]

Wicken revered Nyerere for his integrity and respect for human dignity and equality.

Like her, he rejected conspicuous consumption, and unlike most leaders, he rejected anything that glorified him in any way. Having been to China and having seen the extent to which Mao Tse-tung was

---

[36] Southern African Development Community, of which Tanzania was a member.

[37] Personal correspondence, Joan Wicken to Barbro Johansson, December 26, 1998.

practically worshipped, with ubiquitous photos and statues everywhere, he refused to have such symbols of himself. He even refused to be interviewed for biographies. Nevertheless, his photo did eventually appear in all party headquarters throughout the country, and his likeness was to be found on bank notes and coins. After Nyerere died, a statue of him appeared in Dodoma. However, there was no comparison between these displays of recognition and how some leaders like Joseph Mobutu Sese Seko of Zaire were practically treated like deities.

Wicken was particularly taken by Nyerere's simplicity, which was, of course, her own hallmark. In a eulogy upon his death, she described how in July 1963, he wrote a letter to his ministers and party leaders complaining about grandiosity. He was particularly irritated that when his vehicle drove out of the State House, soldiers would blow the bugle and force traffic off the road. He concluded the letter, which was eventually published, saying: "As a result of this growing insistence on pomposity and ostentation, the President of Tanganyika is fast becoming the worst public nuisance the city of Dar es Salaam has ever had to put up with. It's time it stopped."

When he first became President, Nyerere was given the residence of the previous Governor-General in the State House. Believing it was too grandiose, he borrowed money from the bank and built a small house along the beach in Msasani.[38] The security people built a fence around his home, which he was unhappy about. So he told the government to take over the mortgage and keep the house as government property. He had another four-room home in Butiama he had built for his wife in 1962. He visited this home every Christmas and New Year and eventually retired there.

Wicken appreciated that he was a good listener and listened to anyone he talked to regardless of their position in society. She points out in the interview that he may not have always agreed, but he listened attentively nevertheless. He also arrived at his own judgements and decisions, and he took responsibility for his own decisions. She found him to be well-organised and considerate. He was punctual and did

---

[38] Speech by Ms. Joan Wicken, Personal Assistant to the late Mwalimu Julius K. Nyerere," http://www.southcentre.org/mwalimu/tributes/palaisdesnations/mwalimutributememorialmeeting-10.htm

not complain much. He had difficulty saying no to people.[39]

In her eulogy for Nyerere, she talked about how he was a joyful and lively man. "If you really felt depressed and you had a chance to talk to Mwalimu, you always came back more cheerful. This was not because he thought things were easy — he didn't — nor because he took the easy way out of difficult decisions." She also made the point that "He would say that you are not defeated on anything until you've given up and that the worst sin is despair. The only unforgivable sin, he once told me, is despair. And he took that stance on the unity of Africa and the development of the South and the unity and co-operation of the countries of the South." In the interview and the eulogy, she spoke about how she loved the way he made people laugh when he gave speeches in Swahili at mass rallies. He taught and persuaded with laughter. The only time she saw him angry was when "the dignity of Tanzania or the dignity of individuals was questioned." According to Yahya-Othman, she left the memorial with tears streaming down her cheeks.

---

[39] Correspondence with Powell, 1 July 1984. Nyerere personal Files. Joan Wicken, Cited in Yahya-Othman. p. 175.

At one point, I asked her what Nyerere was most proud of in terms of his accomplishments. She said he was most proud of the peace Tanzania had enjoyed since independence, in spite of the skirmishes with Uganda during Idi Amin's time. He was also proud of the fact that he believed people felt the government was on their side during his presidency. He was pleased with his role in the non-aligned movement and in helping liberate southern Africa. When asked about his main regrets, she said he bitterly regretted sending three men to Zanzibar for questioning after the Zanzibar Revolution. Two were killed in an extrajudicial manner.

Nyerere worked for unity and co-operation in the region, emphasising that it had to come through agreement and persuasion. He worked hard to create an East African Federation but failed, much to his dismay. Nevertheless, he was able to forge a union with Zanzibar in 1964. Wicken reveals in the interview that the union was sacred, and even after he was president, the union was one of the three things he spoke about openly, even though he tried not to interfere too much in the presidency of his successor, Ali Hassan Mwinyi.

From the interview, it is clear that Nyerere's main concerns after stepping down as president in 1990 were the future of Zanzibar's relationship with the mainland, corruption among the country's leaders, and the country losing its sovereignty and self-reliance under pressure for reform from the World Bank and the International Monetary Fund (IMF).

Wicken admired Nyerere for being a proud man who pushed back against pressure from donors, international financial institutions, and foreign countries. He resented any form of dependence and infringement on Tanzania's sovereignty, as was evident when he had to bring in British troops at the 1964 mutiny and in the negotiations with the IMF in the 1980s. It pained him to no end to have to resort to bringing in the British troops, and he did so only as a last resort when it was clear there was no other option.

I asked her about key moments in Tanzania's recent history and how she and Nyerere experienced them. The interview provides a background to their thinking regarding the 1964 Mutiny; the 1964 Zanzibar Revolution; the Union of Tanganyika and Zanzibar; Nyerere's stepping down as president and transition of power to President Mwinyi in 1985;

the liberalization of the economy; the shift towards
multipartyism in the early 1990s, and many other
topics. Many of the facts of these events are known,
but their feelings and thoughts about them are more
explicit in this account than in many others. It details
Nyerere's close relationships with Amir Jamal and his
thoughts about Prime Minister Rashidi Kawawa and
President Hassan Ali Mwinyi.

In spite of their commonalities, Wicken and
Nyerere had some differences. Nyerere was a devout
Catholic who regularly attended mass. Wicken, on
the other hand, was an atheist. In this regard, they
were of different minds, but they did not let these
differences get in the way of their relationship, and
she never made an issue of her religious views.

When I asked about other differences between
her and Nyerere, she mentioned that she opposed
the government closing an organic collective farm
initiative, the Ruvuma Development Association.[40]
Apparently, she also had differences with him on
issues of women's rights. But her general concurrence
with Nyerere probably led her to overlook some of
the stark contradictions between his policies and

---

[40] Yahya-Othman p. 173.

their impact on the very people he purported to care about. Wicken appears at times in the interview to be so eager to defend Nyerere that she not only ignores his paternalism as a leader but also fails to recognise her own patronising comments, for example, when she discusses the women whom she recruited to Kivukoni College ("my women") and when she talked about her co-workers when they did not live up to her expectations.

Limits on Freedom

Throughout the interview, Wicken defends and denies some of the anti-democratic tendencies of the Nyerere era in her effort to carefully curate a certain image of the president. Wicken portrays Nyerere as open to debate and encouraging opposition to his views and as a masterful debater that no one could beat.

Wicken, however, admits at one point that the 1967 Arusha Declaration would not have passed had Tanzania been more democratic: "If we had been as democratic as all that, we would never have got the Arusha Declaration, not because of the people's lack of support, but because of the leadership. Nyerere had to fight that every inch of the way." Indeed, this social contract institutionalising a socialist orientation was framed as a nationalistic project, making it difficult for leaders to reject it.[41] There were purges and a few resignations, including that of Bibi Titi Mohammed, one of the key leaders of the independence movement. Bibi Titi and former foreign minister Oscar Kambona were later accused of plotting to overthrow Nyerere, accusations which landed Bibi Titi in prison after the 1970 treason trial. Kambona had been in London at the time and went into self-exile. The repression of these high profile cases had the effect of silencing open opposition for years to come.

In 1973, Nyerere started implementing his villagisation plan, which involved moving peasants into villages so they could benefit from health and education facilities and engage in collective farming. It involved moving them from their original homes and nearby plots of land to villages, where they were to construct homes in rows, one house next to the other. Peasants were often forcibly removed from their land, causing major havoc to land ownership, the environment, and their livelihoods. From 1973

---

[41] Schneider 2019.

to 1976, over eleven million people were moved to new settlements. My mother, Marja-Liisa Swantz, an anthropologist living and carrying out research in Bunju village north of Dar es Salaam, tape-recorded what Bunju villagers said about villagisation. They talked about the terrible hardships it imposed on them. She took the recordings and played them for Nyerere. His response was typical of how he regarded the entire project of villagisation. He believed that leaders were simply to encourage and educate people to move into these new settlements and that if this did not happen, it meant that leaders were not enforcing the policy properly.[42] It appears he did not take responsibility for the abuses that happened along the way.

On the one hand, it is to Nyerere's credit that he was able to maintain unity within the country at a time when neighbouring countries faced acrimonious divisions along ethnic and religious lines. On the other hand, it came at the price of suppressing civil society and organisations formed along ethnic and religious lines, particularly religious organisations.

---

[42] Schneider, Leander, "Julius Nyerere: Tanzanian President, Statesman, and Intellectual," Oxford, UK: *Oxford Encyclopedia of African History*, 2019.

Moreover, the ruling party increasingly expanded its reach so that most mobilisation around labour, cooperatives, women, youth, and even parents were to be encompassed by party-led mass organisations. The 1962 Preventive Detention Act allowed the government to imprison people deemed threats to the state without going to court. Thus, after the 1964 mutiny of the military, hundreds of labour organisers were arrested under this Act, as were others who were regarded as state security risks.[43]

By 1977, there were 2,000 political detainees in Tanzania, according to Amnesty International.[44]

While there is no way to justify or defend these restrictions on freedom, it is worth noting that despite these acts of repression, Nyerere never came even close to the kinds of wholesale murder of opponents found in Mobutu's Zaire, Mengistu's Ethiopia or Mugabe's Zimbabwe. There is no comparison between Nyerere and most African leaders during his time when it

---

[43] Schneider, 2019.

[44] Nic Cheeseman, Alitalali Amani, Hilary Matfess, "Why we shouldn't expect rapid democratic progress in Tanzania," *Democracy in Africa*, 23 April 2021. http://democracyinafrica. org/why-we-shouldnt-expect-rapid-democratic-progress-in-tanzania/ Accessed June 14, 2021.

came to corruption or the use of state resources for personal gain or the benefit of one's family and kin.

Retirement

In her last years, while living in Keighley, England, Wicken continued to work for the South Commission and then the South Centre, writing speeches for Nyerere. She also spent her time writing up her notes about her work with Nyerere that were to be held in the Bodleian archives, Oxford University. She took up drawing and painting, gave talks on her life and work in Tanzania to groups like Oxfam and a local Third Age Group, consisting of people over 50, who were affiliated with the Third Age University in Keighley. While in Keighley, Wicken began to attend Quaker meetings. She wrote to Barbro Johansson in 1995: "I've also begun some Sundays to attend the Society of Friends (Quaker) Meeting for Worship. Yet I continue to be an atheist! Even so, I find the Silent Hour helpful, and the people there are friendly."[45] She had been introduced to the Quakers through Julia

---

[45] Personal correspondence, Joan Wicken to Barbro Johansson, May 30, 1995.

and Roger Carter while in Tanzania. Roger Carter had gone to Tanzania in 1967 as an adviser to the ministry of education and later worked as a planning officer at the University of Dar es Salaam.[46]

Her hip and back made travel increasingly difficult. She wrote in 1998 to her friend Barbro Johansson, who had retired in Sweden:

> There have sometimes been a few days at the beginning of a break when it was almost physically impossible to get on my feet without help, as well as being in agony to stay there! One of these occurred in China with Mwalimu in 1993 (what a long time ago that now seems!), and on the day that the doctor forgot to take my key with him at night, it took me 15 minutes to get out of bed to open the hotel room door even in my (respectable) pyjamas only! It was that journey that made me finally decide to retire, where instead of me helping Mwalimu, he was worrying about me — and briefing me on his meetings instead of my taking notes etc. Yet I am now so well that I feel guilty about not going back — although I confess that I am positively enjoying not having to work under intense pressure. Also, I have succumbed to the

---

[46] George Penaluna. Joan Wicken 1925 to 2004, The Friend, p. 14. www.thefriend.org/pdfs/050128-thefirend-55.pdf Retrieved online October 31, 2005; Jennifer Donongton, "Obituary: Roger Carter," The Guardian. 8 Feb 2006. https://www.theguardian.com/news/2006/feb/09/obituaries.mainsection

comforts of water reliably from the tap, electricity which does not fail, no horrible insects etc . — as well as a very comfortable chair in which to read, listen to the radio — and doze after lunch! Physically, I could now go back at least half time — but I lack the courage. There is a confession for you. Yet you, in much worse health than me, write about going back to Tanzania! I'm filled with the admiration — and guilt at my own feebleness."[47]

She wistfully ended another letter to Johansson: "My love — and admiration for your courage — comes with this. I, too, wish we could have our old chats: the world is too big. Presumably, it was simpler for those who never left their home village. But what they missed!"[48]

In a 1994 letter to Johansson, she summed up her contributions to Nyerere in this way:

It has been — and is a privilege to be a friend of yours — and to have people asking me if I am Barbro Johansson! In different ways, we have both tried to serve Tanzania and Mwalimu in particular. Our respective successes — and sometimes joint successes — cannot be measured, and we both see some of the things we thought we had achieved broken or disregarded now. Yet, even that doesn't mean what it looks like. In particular, you — and others — see hundreds or thousands of women

---

[47] Personal correspondence, Joan Wicken to Barbro Johansson, December 26, 1998.
[48] Personal correspondence, Joan Wicken to Barbro Johansson, May 30, 1995.

contributing to this country now after being strongly
influenced by you. That cannot be undone. The medal
you received from Mwalimu can be worn with pride. It
was well earned and well received. My love always. We
shall, I hope, meet again. In Sweden, UK, Tanzania or
elsewhere. Look after yourself, please, Joan.[49]

Nyerere's death in 1999 brought an end to the
lifelong collaboration between Wicken and Nyerere.
Wicken herself died of pneumonia after six weeks
of hospitalisation on December 3, 2004, at the age
of 79, in Keighley in West Yorkshire. Joan Wicken's
funeral ceremony was presided over by Maggie
Blunt, a Funeral Officiant of the British Humanist
Foundation, since Wicken did not want a religious
ceremony. The ceremony ended with the playing of
the upbeat New Orleans jazz piece, "Panama Rag" by
Louis Armstrong.

---

[49] Personal communication JoanWicken to Babro Johansson,
March 7, 1994

INTERVIEW WITH JOAN WICKEN

March 3–4, 2000

April 1, 2000

CHILDHOOD AND YOUTH

Her Early Years

AT: What do you remember of your earliest years?

JW: I was born on the edge of London in North Woolwich on July 12, 1925, in a flat. We were poor people. My grandfather[50] was a casual labourer. He collected shrimps and winkles [black shellfish] from the south end of the Thames estuary in his wheelbarrow to sell. He drank the profits. He had five sons, including my father.

My father, Jim Wicken,[51] was the second oldest. My father was basically uneducated. He left school when he was 11. He passed his exam to leave school and went to work with his father. Any education he

---

[50] Her grandfather was William Charles Wicken.

[51] James Wicken was born on April 30, 1894, in East Ham, London.

got after that was from life and from going to evening classes. He never learned ordinary things like where the North and South Downs were.[52] I did ask him once. We had a motorbike and side car at that time, and he fixed it up. We were going over some hill, and I asked him,

"Are these the North Downs or the South Downs?"

He replied:

"What are the Downs, and what do they have to do with us?"

My father sold winkles and shrimps and did odd jobs. At the age of 15 or 16, he worked in a bar. It was there that he started reading. In 1914, he joined the army and survived World War I. He was also taken prisoner. Then he worked in a factory and started taking evening classes at the National Council of Labour Colleges,[53] which was Marxist-run. He was a member of the Workers' Educational Association.[54] By chance, he became a trade union activist. My

---

[52] The North and South Downs are a range of chalk hills that extend along the south eastern coast of England.

[53] The National Council of Labour Colleges was an organization established to promote the education of workers.

[54] The Workers' Educational Association, founded in 1903, is one of Britain's largest charities and a provider of adult education.

father was appointed leader of the Union of Shop, Distributive and Allied Workers.[55]

He met my mother, who was working in a co-op factory, a sugar refining factory that made cakes and sweets and sold them wholesale. She was an organiser of consumer co-ops. In 1922 my parents got married. My mother's maiden name was Lillian Rose Stark.[56] My aunt told me that we lived in a one-bedroom apartment flat facing the church.

I had an older sister, who was born in 1923. Her name was Ivy. I was born in 1925. My mother was sick when my older sister was born. After I was born, she could never lie down in bed again. She had bronchitis and asthma and could not lay down to sleep. Quite clearly, they never had a sexual relationship from that moment on. She was very ill. My entire memory of her was of her being ill, of her gasping for breath. She had better days and worse days. She died when I was seven. But always it was a question of "Mummy

---

[55] He was also involved at some point with the Transport and General Workers' Union and the Trade Union Congress, which is the federation of trade unions in England and Wales that represents the majority of trade unions.

[56] Lillian Rose Stark was born on January 24, 1900, in Woolwich, London.

can't today. Go make the tea or cook the dinner or something." She would do what she could.

My father sent me outside at the age of four to play. We did not have a garden. I went to primary school in Plumstead. He was incredible. When my mother was ill, he made food and tea. He used the treadle sewing machine to make coats for us. My father made pyjamas for my mother in the hospital. When my mother was in the hospital for a year, we were farmed out to other relatives.

She had a sister, my aunt, who visited us to help when my mother was sick. I moved and stayed with my aunt after my mother died. It was a slum, a one small bedroom flat, which I shared with her daughter, Hilda, and her parents.

My father married again after my mother died, and I effectively went back to live with him. Before that, my father did everything. I remember once painting the staircase and ran out of paint, so I added water to the paint and finished the job. My father later asked, "How did you do that without any paint?"

My first political action was in 1937, making a collection for the Spanish Republic and collecting tins of food, which I dutifully handed in. I collected money for Spanish refugee children who were orphans. I was 11 years old and strongly anti-Franco.

I went to a London County Council grammar school when I was around 11; it was an elitist school. They allowed one or two to get in without paying, and I was one of them. I was there when the war broke out. In school, I learned shorthand, bookkeeping and typing. My sister went there as well. Then my sister got a job in a co-op as a shorthand typist in a typing pool. I was 14 when I was evacuated from London to Kent. My father came to get me later. There was a raid, and my school was bombed. Our house was not badly damaged, but the raid was horrible.

I got a job at 14 or 15 typing and doing shorthand at a private garage. I dished out petrol and had to falsify petrol rationing books. I did not have the courage to report them, so I got another job at the London County Council as a clerk. The men were away [presumably as soldiers in the War], and so I got promoted rapidly. As a clerk, I entered who paid. It was a boring job. I asked to be transferred to the County Hall to work in London proper. I was transferred in 1941. It was exciting to work near Westminster. I got a man's job. I was secretary to the deputy education officer.

My sister died in 1941 at the age of 19 from tuberculosis and meningitis. It had a big impact on me as we had always been together. One day [when we were together in London] there was an air raid warning. I stopped at the nearest air raid shelter and jumped in. The bomb blasted and threw her on the ground. She was in a lot of pain.

I remember cutting my hair short because it felt so heavy. She was much prettier than I was, with wavy hair that was red. I loved it, and she didn't. I was the dead spitting image of my father insofar as a woman can be. Janet, my half-sister, looked like me. Ivy, my sister, looked like my mother.

I never did what my father said, which wore down on him. My aunt said I was a great disappointment as I was intended to be a boy and that I looked like my father.

During the War, I joined the army anti-aircraft Auxiliary Territorial Service[57] and was placed on guns and radar training. I was the first-ever operator of radar. It was very secret, and I was very inefficient.

---

[57] The Women's branch of the British Army during World War II. It was initially a voluntary service and existed from 1938 to 1949, when it was merged into the Women's Royal Army Corps.

But we did feel we were contributing even though the only plane we got down was one of our own. The recognition signal did not work. It was not a direct hit, and no one died. I was not on duty.

By the time I was an operative, they [the Germans] were using V-1s and V-2s[58] — pilotless missiles shaped like airplanes propelled by fire. I was stationed at Kensington Ashford near the coast. The V-1s and V-2s had such a speed, the only hope was to get guns onto it when it had passed over us. The people of Ashford didn't want us taking them down over them. By the end of 1944, I applied to go overseas. Antwerp [Belgium] had the same problem with V-1s and V-2s being too fast [to take down]. I stayed there until V-day. I went to the typing [pool] and worked with the American army for six weeks. It took all that time to get used to their food. I was posted to Germany until I was demobed [demobilised] in 1947, two years

---

[58] V-weapons were long-range artillery weapons used by the Germans in World War II in 1944–45 against the British. V-1 was a pulsejet-powered cruise missile while the V-2 was a liquid-fueled ballistic missile. The V-weapon offensive ended in March 1945. The last V-2 attack was in Kent March 27, 1945, and the last attack of any kind on British soil took place a few days later on March 29.

later. There was no fraternisation with the Germans, so I did not learn German in the typing pool, where I remained until I got appendicitis. A commanding officer came in and asked me how I was, and I said, "not good." I was put into a smaller office and then demobed.

AT: Could you talk more about the influence of your father on you?

JW: I was brought up by my father. My father was a clever man with no opportunity. In one of my earliest political memories, I remember him saying to me that income tax is the only fair tax there is because you pay tax according to what you have. It is silly to say you are going to take half of somebody's income. If you take half of somebody's income, they barely have enough to live on. Then you are killing him. But if he is really rich, you hardly notice. I remember seeing a cartoon; heaven knows what paper it was in, either the *Daily Herald* or it might have been the *Daily Worker*. There were one or two trade union magazines coming into the house. I can remember seeing this cartoon of a ladder coming up a river, and people were standing at various rungs. The man at the bottom has the water up to his chin, and the man at the top did not get his feet wet, and he said,

"We will be fair. We will all take one step down."

It was obvious, the one at the bottom was going to have his nose and mouth below the water.

My father was a member of the Labour Party. I remember when my sister and I were very small, it was a great treat during elections to go around and distribute election leaflets to people's doors. It was never a job. It was always something you knew, if you were very good, "I'll let you do this." I remember also when I was 13 or 14, I went to some gathering and met a young boy there. He was talking about the Young Communist League, and [he asked me if I] would like to come along [to a meeting of the League].

I said, "Yes, it would be a good idea."

I told my father about this, and he said, "Do as you like, but they will only laugh at you. You are too young."

I was much more terrified of being laughed at than anything else, so I didn't go.

In commitment and in fairness, and in doing his job, he was a marvellous person, my father. My father used to work in a factory that was some distance away, and he would leave home at about 6:30 am and get home at about 6:30 pm. Then he would set about and do whatever she [my mother] could not do, including having a bath once a week. [He would] take a bucket outside and fill it with water. He did everything he could do, whatever was necessary. He was a good man and also a very intelligent man. He was active. He could not be very active in the trade unions when she was alive because he couldn't be both at the meeting of the party or the trade union and getting home to do all that was necessary.

I remember these things, and they made an impact on me.

There used to be newspapers. I can't remember which one I got this from, but they were talking about the Germans as Huns, and I asked,

"Why do they call the Germans Huns?"

He [my father] was telling me about the war and somebody saying how bad the Germans were. I remember this vaguely. He said,

"If you saw a German walking down the street, you wouldn't know he is German. He is just like everybody else. All people the world over are the same."

My mother was a Methodist. He [my father] wasn't anything; he was an agnostic. He said if there was a god —I asked him about this once—he didn't need you to go telling him how good he was because he knew that already. But he wanted you to behave yourself. Do good things. In a sense, Methodists were a strong element in the Labour Party. I never got it [a religious upbringing]; because I stopped going to Sunday School to give my mother a break [with chores] on Sunday afternoons.

When he [my father] got the money to buy the [motor]cycle, with the help of his brother, he converted the cycle [to include a sidecar] so that he could get my mother in the front and the two girls in the back. Then we would go out for trips on Sunday afternoons if my mother was fit. But he was really a marvellous person.

So, in a sense, you could say my father taught me and got me interested in politics. I started arguing with people about politics. I didn't know what economics was, and I decided I had to learn this. During the war, I started doing correspondence courses. Evening classes didn't take place at all because of the war. Also, when I was in the army, I did a correspondence course. I did economics, and I had done English before that. It just so happened that they used to subcontract these correspondence courses, and one was subcontracted to Ruskin College.[59] That is how I learned about Ruskin College at the time. When I got demobed [demobilised], I told my father that I wanted to go to Oxford. He was very much against me going to college. I asked why he was against it, and he said,

"Because you will forget your class."

Ruskin College (1947–1949)

AT: You went to Ruskin College for two years?

JW: Yeah. From 1947 to 1949, I was at Ruskin.

AT: What did you study there?

JW: I studied a bit of everything because remember, I really didn't have very much, so I did some economics, a bit of politics, very basic stuff. Reading the odd political philosopher like Rousseau and a few others like that. Ruskin certainly didn't do anything further than that. It is a labour college. It is still there,

---

[59] Ruskin College is an independent educational institution based in Oxford with links to the Univerity of Oxford. It provides educational opportunities for adults, often with few or no formal qualifications, who have been marginalized in some way but who want to make a difference in the world.

but it is getting somewhat reflective of Mrs Thatcher, shall I say. It was a college closely linked with the labour movement, so the trade unions at that time paid for quite a large proportion of its income. The scholarship I had was for working women, and it had been paid for by some group of trade unions. I don't know which one, but they were concerned about women, so it was a women's scholarship. Most people [students], not everybody, most had trade union backgrounds or cooperative backgrounds, or a Labour [Party] background. But you have to remember that during the six years of war [World War II], there had not been any political activity. I didn't join during the War as I could have done because we were in a coalition government, and I didn't see the point of that. I volunteered to join the forces.[60] I was very patriotic, and I sort of basically saw that we were being bombed and wanted to hit back. I joined the Labour Party as soon as I got demobed [demobilised]. I have been a member ever since, except when I was in Tanzania. At that point, you couldn't be a member if you were abroad.

---

[60] Auxiliary Territorial Service.

Labour Party Organiser (1949–1951)

JW: From 1949 to 1951, I was a Labour Party organiser in Gloucestershire, a rural constituency. We had a Labour MP [member of parliament] when I got there. He was elected in 1945. We had a Tory MP when I left two years later [laughter], but only by 27 votes, which, considering it was a traditional Tory seat, it wasn't bad: a 27-vote majority out of 67,000 votes. That was in the 1950 election. I had just been there a year. I had a tremendous reputation as an agent because I took over from somebody who had been falsifying the books, so perhaps I managed to sort them out and get them right. We did so well in that election. We weren't expected to win. The other thing was I thought we would win, but that was just me. I enjoyed that job. It was tough, and there were very few women organisers. The chairman had disapproved of the idea from start to finish. But, as I said, I was honest, and he forgave me a lot for that. The chairman was very good. He tried very hard to conceal from me [that] he didn't want me there. But anyway, I was there for two years.

Somerville College, University of Oxford (1951–1953)

AT: When were you at school then?

JW: It was only a two-year course at Ruskin [College]. After 1951, I went to Somerville [College, University of Oxford]. I got a scholarship. The Labour government had introduced scholarships for mature students, [again] for which you had to have no qualifications. You did an essay. I think there were 40 [scholarships] each year, and I got one of them, and I wasn't terribly sure I wanted to go by that time. I decided I must try for the state scholarship for mature students, and I did that and then got the Somerville.[61] My father didn't object, and I think he thought I was pretty secure in my loyalties.

Somerville was at Oxford, just across the road from Ruskin. At that time, I had the scholarship, but you had to fix your own arrangement, your place to put up. By that time, I wasn't at all sure I wanted to go back to do more study. So, I just made it difficult for myself deliberately. Somerville had a reputation of being very concerned about academic standards.

---

[61] Somerville College was one of the Oxford University's first two women's colleges.

That wasn't my purpose. My purpose was to learn more economics. I then did PPE: politics, philosophy and economics. It is the only way they taught it.

From Ruskin, you don't get a degree, so this [the degree from Somerville College] was an undergraduate degree. I was accepted there [at Somerville], but I then decided I wanted to do the degree in two years and not in three. I knew that some people from Ruskin had done it. To the very end, Somerville tried to persuade me to do more. The question was should I go, but they said I would go down to third class. Eventually, I did go. We had a class system. Oxford didn't have the upper and lower second, they just had third, second and first. I said I don't care if I get a third. I want to learn economics and not worry about a degree. Anyway, in the end, because they were so insistent that I would go down a class, the only way to prove that wasn't true was to get a first. But I didn't. I got a second. At least it wasn't a third. I was able to basically carry on and do the course in two years [1951–1953]. I took the Oxford University diploma in political science and economics, and I got that with distinction, which was important only in that it helped me later.

Why I wanted to go at all was because I had been through an election, and we had to have a lot of meetings in scattered areas, and the candidate would be addressing three meetings a night, at least. My part of my job was to go to the first one and make sure everything was in order. Then I had to get that going and make sure they had speakers to go on until the candidate arrived. If there was not a problem with the first one, then I would leave that one and go on to the next one. Again, if something went wrong, I would have to stand up and speak.

On one occasion, I stood up and spoke, and there was a heckler. I remember he asked me about devaluation. The Labour government had devalued [the currency] in 1949, and you know it was held very much against them. Anyway, they had to devalue, and, you see, I thought I knew the answer to that question. I knew the principle: you ignore a heckler if you can't answer him. If you can, you squash him, and I thought I could squash him. But he knew much more about devaluation than I did [laughter]. I was deeply in a terrible mess when the candidate arrived, and I was never so pleased to see him. I decided I had better go and learn some more economics. I decided to go for this scholarship for mature students, and I got it.

I then decided, first I was going to Oxford [University] and nowhere else. If I couldn't go to Oxford, I would give it up. Having been accepted, I then had to get into a college, and, again, I was still not very sure. Somerville [College] had a reputation of being very difficult to get into and [of having] a very high academic sort of status, so I decided I'd want to go to Somerville. In fact, it was good academically. It had a marvellous principal, Dr Janet Vaughan, and she was a socialist and a medical doctor. She was still doing research in the college as well as serving on various university committees. She was interested in having somebody unusual, so she accepted me. She had a habit every term of interviewing every student in the college. But for some reason, most of the students were terrified of this. Most of the interviews lasted about two minutes. Mine always lasted at least 15 [minutes] because we would get talking. I remember her telling me once,

"You really found out who your friends are when you have been talking in Hyde Park [speakers] corner[62] and then walk along Oxford Street only to

---

[62] Hyde Park Speakers corner was a site in London allocated by parliament for public speaking. Anyone could turn up unannounced and speak on any subject considered lawful. It

find that some of your friends cross over to the other side [of the street]."

Vaughan had also been to the concentration camps [in Germany] when they were taken over [at the end of World War II] because she was doing research about blood and defects of malnutrition and starvation. So, she went to two or three of those [camps] when they were first taken back.[63] She was a fantastic person. Anyway, it was really because of her I got in. Then I decided I wanted to do the course [program] in two years and not three. She said, "no." Everybody said "no." But you see, then I had come up late because of the 1951 election. You couldn't walk out of an election to go to college, so I came up three weeks late.

My successor was already there. Then they said to me:

"Which are you going to take in prelims, French or math?"

....

is the location of many protests and demonstrations on the northeast edge of Hyde Park. Karl Marx, Vladimir Lenin and George Orwell are among the best-known speakers.

[63] Vaughan went to the Bergen-Belsen concentration camp in Germany and succeeded in improving efforts to feed people suffering from extreme starvation.

I replied, "First off, what are prelims?" That is an exam you have to take after two terms. "Fine. What [do] you mean? I can't do French or math," I asked.

"You must have been able to," said my tutor. "How did you get here without French or math?" asked the tutor [laughter]. She continued, "You had other subjects, but those two were compulsory."

"But you accepted me!" I replied. [laughter] "You didn't ask those questions."

They discovered that when I had been at this grammar school, I had done some French before I was 14. They said:

"Ah, we will give you private tuition [lessons]."

I said, "Look, when I went to this school, we had end of year exams, and I failed every one in French."

"No, no, that will be alright."

They were really helpful. They sent me to a private tutor for French. At the end of the first term, she sent a message back:

"This woman will never learn French in a thousand years, much less in two terms. Now, what do we do with her?" [laughter]

They said I could get an exemption because I got distinction in the diploma. Because they didn't see any other choice, I got an exemption. Even then, they sort of still made conditions. They were hopeful. They said I mustn't work during the vacation, and I said my grant was not sufficient, so they arranged for me to stay at the college most of the time. In return for board and lodging, I would go and work in the kitchens for a couple of hours a day or something. So, I accepted that.

EARLY CAREER

Assistant Commonwealth Officer (1953–1959)

JW: By luck, I applied for a job in 1953, which was advertised in the Commonwealth Department of the Labour Party, and I got it: Assistant Commonwealth Officer. It sounded very grand, but there was just the commonwealth officer and me, which wasn't very grand. But anyway, I enjoyed it. I worked there until 1959.

The Commonwealth Office was at the Labour Party headquarters. It was all part of colonial affairs. Our job was to promote Labour Party policy, which, of course, was, in principle, the independence of colonial countries. Then we had to, you know, try to educate people. We used to write articles in the Labour Party press and the internal journal.

Occasionally, we would do something for the Fabian Society[64] journal, *Venture*.

While I was there [at the Commonwealth Office], Mwalimu came to visit the Labour Party on his first visit in 1955, and my boss was on a trip to the Caribbean. So, they phoned me [up] from the Enquiry office and said,

"We have a man here who wants to see John Hatch."[65]

I asked, "What is his name?"

"We can't pronounce his name."

AT: So, John Hatch was the Commonwealth Officer at that time?

JW: Yes. He wasn't when I first went, but he was then. So, I asked,

"Where does he come from?"

"Tanganyika."

"Is his name Julius Nyerere?"

---

[64] The Fabian Society was founded in 1884 in Britain as a socialist organisation with the purpose of advancing the principles of democratic socialism rather than revolutionary overthrow.

[65] John Hatch was a Commonwealth Secretary of the Labour Party in the 1950s. He also was Commonwealth correspondent for the *New Statesman* and later served as a policy advisor to Tanzania's President Julius Nyerere and Zambia's President Kenneth Kaunda.

"It could be."

"Look, tell him to wait there. I'm coming down."

And it was Julius Nyerere. Because my boss was away, I was able to take him around and introduce him to members of parliament and take him to Labour Party meetings.

He used to come to Labour Party meetings and listen to me make speeches, which made me laugh later when I saw what his speeches were like and what his audience was like. We used to get requests from local parties. Somebody from the State or Transport House [asked us] to come down to speak at a Labour Party meeting on something, so I was doing some of that. He came with me to several of those. He used to sit there and always refused to say anything. I remember one time we had 40 people at that meeting, and I said to him,

"That was a good meeting, wasn't it?"

Forty people at a Labour Party meeting, it was quite good.

I got to know Tom Mboya[66] very well because he was at Ruskin, but not while I was there. He was at

---

[66] Tom Mboya (1930–1969) was a Kenyan trade unionist, independence activist, and politician. He led the negotiations for Kenya's independence at Lancaster House and was one of the

Ruskin later on. But then, through contacts, I met him, and we got along fine. In fact, John did not like my being in contact with him.

AT: Why?

JW: Least of all, he thought he should be dealing with him. John Hatch tended to deal with Kenya more. I got a letter from Tom once. I don't know how he [John] learned about that anyway, and he wanted to see it. I refused to give it to him, and we had a big row about that. I finally left, not really because of [the incident regarding] Tom, but because of the whole attitude at the office, the attitude toward me, basically. I mean, I didn't like him [John Hatch] either, to tell the truth. I thought he was good when he first came in. I always felt that he was as concerned to promote himself as he was to promote what we were supposed to be doing. I was also getting on in my late 20s. He had been very angry not knowing that Julius was

....

founders of the Kenya African National Union that led Kenya to independence. He served as its first secretary general. In 1955, he received a scholarship from the British Trades Union Congress to attend Ruskin College, where he studied industrial management. He held numerous ministerial positions. He met an untimely death at the age of 38, when he was assassinated in what was widely believed to be a political assassination.

coming and was a bit upset to find out that I had been taking him [Nyerere] out and that I was going to see him the next year in Tanganyika.

Anyway, I knew Tom and Julius, of course. You know, in 1955, he [John Hatch] went out to Tanganyika and the mass meetings that he addressed made a tremendous impression on him.

On the Alice Horsman Traveling Fellowship in Africa (1956–1957)

While I was there [at the Labour Party Commonwealth Office], I applied for this Alice Horsman Traveling Fellowship from Somerville.[67] I talked [to Nyerere] about my plans with this fellowship. My original plan was to go to Kenya and then the Central African Federation [Federation of Rhodesia and Nyasaland], and then Ghana. Mwalimu asked:

"How are you going to get from Kenya to Nyasaland?"

---

[67] See more: Wicken, Joan E. 1958. "African Contrasts." Unpublished report of Alice Horsman Travelling Fellow, 1956–7. Bodleian Library of Commonwealth and African Studies at Rhodes House, Oxford University, Mss.Afr.s172b.

"Oh, there must be buses or something. I'll find out," I replied.

"Anyway," he said, "you have got to cross Tanganyika, so you come and be our guest."

So, I was the guest of TANU for three weeks. And wherever I went, I was interviewing African scholars for Ruskin. I talked to Lucy Lameck[68] and three other people in Tanganyika. I asked Julius,

"Look, I've talked to these four, and I know what my inclination is, but they are all TANU members. Which one is going to be most useful?"

"They should all go," he replied.

I said, "Come on, you should talk sense; you'll only get one if you're lucky."

"They should all go."

"Look, that is no good."

"What we need," he said, "is a college like Ruskin in Dar es Salaam."

---

[68] Lucy Lameck (1934–1993) attended Ruskin College. She was appointed to the Tanganyikan National Assembly (parliament) in 1960, where she served until 1992, except for a break during the years 1975 to 1980. She served as Parliamentary Secretary of Cooperatives and Community Development between 1962–1965, making her the first woman in Tanganyika to hold such a high ministerial post.

So, I said to him, "Fine, brilliant idea, but let's get on with reality; which one do you want to go [to]?"

I can't remember; he never did answer that question. I went ahead on my own anyway. Of course, from my mind, it was obvious that the only woman that was applying on my list, Lucy [Lameck], was obviously capable [and she was selected]. I take no credit for this. I wasn't doing anything in particular. I was just doing my job. Anyway, that was in 1957.

The first African election was on while I was in Kenya. I attended and somehow or another got involved in that. It was a bit difficult because when I arrived, there were crowds of people all around this building. I think there was a count going on. I arrived all on my own, and I am a white woman coming into this place. But anyway, Tom [Mboya] must have anticipated that I might be having trouble, so he sent somebody out to look for me. So, they rescued me. I knew Tom well, and we got along well.

And I went on from there to Tanganyika. I saw Lucy [Lameck] in Moshi. I didn't stay there long, a couple of days, I suppose. Then I got the bus down to Dar es Salaam, where Mwalimu and a couple of friends, colleagues met me [off the bus]. Then I travelled with him and six other African members of

TANU in a jeep down to Mbeya, spending the night
in Iringa. I flew from there to Lilongwe [in Malawi]
and went down to Blantyre [in Malawi] by bus. Then I
flew over to Southern Rhodesia, where I was rescued
there. I had gone to some hotel in Salisbury.

Anyway, fortunately, the next day I met a man
called Zelta. His wife was away, but he said I could
come and stay in their house. He lent me his driver
and his car if I needed to go to someplace. From
there, I went to some friends' farm where I met Guy
and Molly Clutton-Brock.[69] Do you know them? Guy
and his wife Molly had started the farm. He turned
out to be a farm manager of this mission farm, but

---

[69] Arthur Guy Clutton-Brock (1906–1995) and his wife Molly
Clutton-Brock moved from Britain to Southern Rhodesia
(known after independence as Zimbabwe). He was an
agricultural demonstrator and missionary. He co-founded Cold
Comfort Farm in Zimbabwe. Guy Clutton-Brock helped form the
Southern Rhodesia African National Congress in 1957, which
promoted partnership policies between Blacks and Whites. He
was detained without trial in 1959 and in 1971 he and his wife
were deported by the Ian Smith government. After his death he
was declared a national hero by the Government of Zimbabwe.

in fact, he converted it into an African cooperative.[70]
It was [originally] called St. Francis [sic St. Faith's
Mission]. Then he was thrown out. He was first
imprisoned, then he was taken into detention, and
then he was thrown out [of Rhodesia]. But he became
a Rhodesian, so they couldn't get rid of him. He
came back [to Rhodesia], and he then started Cold
Comfort Farm, which is a cooperative.

There was no doubt at all; a lot of freedom fighters
were transiting through these places and staying
there for some time. When he was put in prison, the
church got back his house. Because it was a European
area, it had to be registered in his name and some
other people's name, including Guy's and his wife's
names. It was known as a cooperative and governed
by the members. I just spent the one night there, and
I stayed with Molly and Guy in a caravan. That is
where I slept. When we came back, I asked the driver,

"How was it for you? Were you alright?"

"They were just like ordinary people," he replied.

"What do you mean?" I queried.

---

[70] Cold Comfort Farm was a multiracial cooperative community
in Rusape, founded in and closed down by the government in
1971.

"Well, we all ate together, and there was some table tennis, and we all played table tennis."

AT: How did this trip [to Africa in 1956–1957] affect you? How did it shape you?

JW: It convinced me that I would like to go back to Africa to do something useful if there was something useful I could do. But certainly, the country I would like to go back to was Tanganyika. Partly because of the different atmosphere. Nyasaland was horrible because it was a federation at the time, and there was this [racial] separation. It wasn't apartheid, but it was difficult to see what the difference was. Rhodesia for the same reason and northern Rhodesia I thought was also suffering from that, but also it was a rather violent society, and I am a coward. I don't like violence.

West Africa, I enjoyed and loved, but they are very effervescent. The other [countries I visited] all had the strong influence of the settlers. I stopped off in Nigeria because I knew some people there. They had been students when I was in the Labour Party. Lagos was just horrible. Lagos is always horrible. I mean, it is the climate, for one thing. But you know they are a very effervescent people. Despite all those years, I still found it very difficult to be excited in public. My sort of tight, stiff upper lip philosophy is still very much with me even though I am not as bad as I once was. But I still found it very difficult. I could like it and recognise that it was Africa, but I couldn't see myself fitting into it.

I liked Tanganyika, which was much more gentle. I mean, the crowds were huge and could get very excited. I went to see Mwalimu speak, and when he was in charge of these crowds, he made them laugh. He told them stories. He told them what was wrong, why they needed independence, and what they could do if they were independent.

I mean, he was adamant and hot against these colonialists, but it wasn't against the individuals. He would make that point time and time again. Also, he would make them laugh, so it wasn't an angry crowd when I was there. The only time I saw it like that was when [Malawi's Hastings] Banda[71] came

---

[71] Hastings Kamuzu Banda (1905–1997) was appointed Prime Minister of Nyasaland and led the country to independence in 1964. In 1966, the country became the Republic of Malawi, and Banda became president of this repressive autocracy. He ruled from 1964 to 1994. Banda declared a one-party state and in 1970 he was made President for Life of the ruling Malawi Congress Party and President for Life of Malawi in 1971.

through [Tanganyika], and he came through just after the breakup of the federation.[72] He made a speech in English, of course, and it was translated by [Kanyama] Chiume.[73] Chiume certainly added enough pepper to that translation. I knew enough Swahili to see what he was doing. But the audience got quite angry. The atmosphere was very different.

I mean, he was very bitter. It just made it a different audience. Because you know crowds can be worked up one way or the other. This is a huge crowd in Mnazi

---

[72] The Federation of Rhodesia and Nyasaland was a colonial federation (1953–1963) made up of Southern Rhodesia (Zimbabwe after 1980) and the British protectorates of Northern Rhodesia (Zambia after 1964) and Nyasaland (Malawi after 1964).

[73] Kanyama Chiume (1929–2007) was a leading nationalist in Malawi's independence movement in the 1950s and 1960s. He grew up with his uncle in Tanzania and studied at Makerere College before returning to Malawi to fight for independence. He was a leader of the Nyasaland African Congress (which eventually became the Malawi Congress Party) and served as the Minister of Education and the Minister for Foreign Affairs. He was forced into exile by the Hastings Banda regime after being at the center of the 1964 Cabinet Crisis in which he opposed Banda. He remained in Tanzania from 1964-1994 and eventually moved to New York.

Mmoja.[74] They moved the mass meetings from Mnazi Mmoja to Jangwani. I don't know why they did this. They had done it before I got there. Maybe the sheer numbers in size. But anyway, it was a very different atmosphere that meeting. Quite often I would just go either alone or with one or two other people, black or white, sometimes Roland Brown, for example. You never felt threatened, nor [did you feel that] people were eyeing you suspiciously, but you did that day. I wasn't doing anything different than I did on any other days.

Mwalimu was there, of course. Before the end of the meeting, he stood up and made some jokes. I can't remember them. Indeed, his jokes were one thing I didn't always get in Swahili. He calmed the crowd down, basically. This was before independence because I was there in April 1960, and December 1961 was independence. Kivukoni had already opened by then.

---

[74] Mnazi Mmoja is a large park in Dar es Salaam near Kariakoo used for public gathering.

Working with the Africa Education Trust (1957–1960)

AT: Is it true that you started Kivukoni College?

JW: That is what I went out for. I went back to work for the Labour Party's International Department, but it was called the Commonwealth Office. Technically, I was called the assistant commonwealth officer, but it wasn't ever called the Commonwealth Office. There were just two of us. We even shared an office. I left the Labour Party in 1959 because I could not stand working with John Hatch anymore, but they were very good to me. The secretary general of the Labour Party didn't like Hatch, but for different reasons. The Labour Party were terrible payers. But anyway, he [the secretary general] said:

"Look, when you go to your next job, what you get will depend on what you get now." He asked, "What are you earning now?"

"£750 a year," I replied.

He said, "I will increase your salary to £850 for the remaining months or whatever it takes until you get a job, and you can tell them that is your salary."

This is what I did. I went to become the first secretary ever of the Africa Education Trust, which is still going now. I was extremely bad. I was the wrong sort of person for that job. At least I got it launched, and I didn't do any lasting harm. I did my best, but I wasn't quite sure what I was supposed to be doing.

AT: Where was this?

JW: In London.

AT: What did it do? Sponsor fellowships?

JW: It didn't start that way, but it does that now. At that time, the idea was that we were going to be promoting primary and secondary education in Africa. We were also going to bring out [publish] some booklets on various issues of policy, like educational policy in Africa. I think we did bring out two while I was there. I am not even sure about that. I honestly can't remember much about it.

AT: Was this a Labour Party organisation?

JW: No, no, not at all. Do you know anything about Rev. Michael Scott, who started the Africa Bureau?[75]

---

[75] Michael Scott (1907–1983) was an Anglican priest in Britain, known for his anti-apartheid advocacy. In 1943 he moved to Johannesburg, South Africa, to serve as chaplain. He became the first white man to be jailed for protesting the country's racial laws. In 1952 he co-founded the Africa Bureau, which supported Africans in their constitutional pursuit of independence. He was also known for his advocacy around Namibia's independence

He was originally in South Africa as a priest, and he was not Huddlestone,[76] but in a different sort of way, very much on the African side. [Representatives of] the Herero people from Namibia, from South West Africa, asked him to come and see them and [learn about their plight]. He was then thrown out from South Africa, declared a persona non grata and told to get out. He did not belong to any kind of order, so he did not get much publicity, and nobody in Britain wanted him. He was a saintly figure, much more so than Trevor, whom I knew and liked very much, but Michael was rather saintly and unworldly, but definitely saintly. I liked him and knew him very well. He went and spoke for the Herero several times at the UN Trusteeship Council and went on doing that for quite some time. He had been away for so long. He

....

from South Africa and was an early advocate of nuclear disarmament.

[76] Trevor Huddleston (1913–1998) was a British Anglican bishop. He became the second Archbishop of the Church of the Province of the Indian Ocean. He was known for his anti-apartheid activism. From 1960-68 he served as Bishop of Masasi in Tanzania, where he re-organised the mission schools, which were taken over by the government. He was a good friend of Nyerere's.

couldn't go back to [Namibia] even to report on what he had been doing.

He had set up the Africa Bureau in London, a non-governmental organisation. He was trying to give African leaders some help in lobbying and publicity. They [the members of the Africa Bureau] were all party members of the Labour Party, but it was rather a sort of educated middle-class organisation. I have a great friend, Jane Kellogg; she was then Jane Simons. She was the head of it when I went there. The Africa Education Trust was sort of, in a sense, an offshoot of that.

Establishing Kivukoni College (1960–1961)

JW: In about March of 1958, I got a letter from Julius, in which he said that at the [TANU] party congress in Tabora in February 1958, there was tremendous conflict about whether or not they should take part in the multiparty elections, you know, three candidates for each seat. Sometime in the middle, they passed a resolution to set up in Dar es Salaam a college like Ruskin College [laughter]. So, of course, I jumped onto this and started collecting adult education

constitutions in Britain and sending my bright ideas
and so on and so forth. Then I discovered that one of
the difficulties was that the colonial government was
saying that they couldn't do it. Why? Because they
were frightened of another Mau Mau.

"You see [the impact of the] independent colleges
of Kenya," they said.

So, I got this raised in various articles [in the UK]
about Kivukoni with a number of MPs. It was raised
in parliament or through MPs in government.

Then Julius came through London on his way to
the [United] States in late 1959. He found me in the
Africa Education Trust, so, of course, I wanted to
know what was happening with the college. He told
me they had bought this derelict hotel, which was
quite contrary to the advice I had given them, but
anyway, they had done it. They got stuck because they
didn't have anybody who knew anything about adult
education who had the time to do anything about it.
To cut a long story short, we agreed that I would come,
and we went together to the Noel Buxton Trust.[77]

---

[77] The Noel Buxton Trust was established by Noel Edward Buxton
in 1919 to promote social and economic progress in Britain and
throughout the world. Today it focuses on subSaharan Africa.

Noel Buxton[78] had been an earlier socialist. I think
he had been an MP at one time, a rather unorthodox
maverick type of person, but well-known. I think
he was a pacifist, not in the mainstream, but well-
known, highly respected. Somehow, he had this little
Trust. It was a very little one, and we went to them,
and they agreed to pay my fare one way. I accepted.

I wrote letters to them [colonial government]; no
one ever answered them. I know why now, of course,
but at the time, it was disconcerting [that] nobody
answered my letters. I think in March, I got a letter
asking, "Why aren't you here?" This wasn't sent by
Mwalimu; it was sent by Mahmoud N. Rattansey,
who was the secretary. We always called him Madia.
Rattansey was an Asian.

What had they done? They had got around the
problem with the government in the end. I don't
know how they were advised to do this. They set
up a charitable trust, which had on it 13 members:
three Asian, three European or whites — all of whom
were settlers, or businessmen — seven Africans

---

[78] Noel Buxton (1869–1948) was a British Liberal Party and later
Labour Party politician. He served as Minister of Agriculture and
Fisheries under Ramsay MacDonald.

and Mwalimu as chairman. It was a nonpolitical, nonsectarian, nonreligious, non-everything charitable trust set up to establish a college along the lines of Ruskin College. You see, nobody knew what Ruskin College was. So then, as I discovered much later — Mwalimu didn't tell me at the time — he was told when he went to London to find somebody who would come out as secretary/principal of the school. He never told me that at all. He asked me to come out as secretary of this trust. The word principal was not mentioned, and it never was mentioned until after I had been there for donkeys' years and the college was opened that I discovered this instruction [laughter]. By that time, Colin Leys[79] was the principal.

So, I went out [to Tanganyika] on the 9th of April 1960. It was great fun. It was marvellous coming there. They showed me where the place [for Kivukoni College] was across the harbour. We had to fight our way through the bush because, of course, the bush

---

[79] Colin Leys is a British political economist who was principal of Kivukoni College from 1960 to 1962. He taught at Balliol College, Oxford University, from 1956–1960 before going to Kivukoni. He then held chairs at Uganda's Makerere University and universities in Sussex, Nairobi and Sheffield and was a professor at Queens University in Canada.

had grown up around the hotel. It had been a hotel, I think three times, but it had always gone bankrupt because of communication.[80]

AT: Who had owned it?

JW: Private people. I have no idea who had owned it.[81] Anyway, it was a small hotel, a very nice one, with an open square with a courtyard. You could see the harbour from most of the rooms, but, of course, it was derelict, so we had to cut the bush to get there. The TANU Youth League came in and did that. We had to get an architect to come in and look and see if it was structurally safe, and they reckoned it was. We had to redo the roof because it was leaking like mad, and I found some rusty bedsteads and the odd chair. Anyway, there were plenty of taps around and electricity. Of course, we discovered the electricity needed rewiring. But you know it seemed to me that if you've got taps, you've got water. I'm a Londoner. After we had been getting it repaired and built up, opened up and even rewired, somebody in town, I don't know who it was, asked me,

---

[80] It previously had been the Bel Air Hotel, then Ghana Holiday Hotel and eventually the Dolphin Hotel.

[81] They bought if from Sayani & Company.

"What about the water?"

I said, "Sorry, I'm a Londoner. I haven't thought about this. I don't know. I will have to go and look."

I found that the pipes came from a well. Probably the same person said,

"You should get a medical officer to come [and] look at that water."

"Should I?"

"Well," he said, "Of course, you should."

I got a medical officer from the City Council, and he came. He sent his report, which stated: "For the first time in my life, I have encountered typhoid germs coming out of a tap." It was a bit late. We were almost about to open. But it was certainly too late to do anything major or structural. The thing was solved by getting a new tank on top and while the other work was being done, shovelling chlorine in every day. Anyway, we all survived, and nobody got sick.

AT: How did you get there? By ferry?

JW: By ferry. But while this was being done, we did work hard. I got a car by that time, a Peugeot 403. I mean, I was ashamed, you know. I said to [someone on the Kivukoni trust]:

"You can't spend your money on a big car for me."

"I thought you are going up country?" he replied.

"Well, I am."

"You will need that car if you don't need something else stronger, bigger," he continued.

Anyway, I started organising in June or July and went up to the Lake Region. The regional party office organised visits for me to districts and from districts down to villages to talk about Kivukoni and collect money from the people.

First, you have to get permission from the police to collect money. At first, they refused, asking,

"How are you going to do this?"

"We are going to have collection boxes," I replied.

"Collection boxes can be opened. You can just put your hand in and take the money out."

"Well, we are collecting for the college."

We had to find some other means for collecting. [We came up with] a metal box that didn't have any means of opening the box at all except with a tin opener. That was it. That was that, solved. Basically, I was working for TANU. This was before independence in 1960. Mwalimu gave me a TANU driver, Said Kamtawa. A fine person. He didn't know any English, and I didn't know any Swahili at that point. But anyhow, we managed. He got quite excited about the college in the end. I was going to meet the committee when I arrived at a district. He would be outside talking to a crowd who had come to see what this was all about, telling them all about the college.

We drove the first time up to Lake District, starting in Sukumaland, where they had recently had a cotton harvest, and so they had some money. On the first day in the District TANU office, the TANU Youth League would fill the car [with collection boxes]. I saw why I had to have a big car. Because except for my seat and the drivers' seat, the place was filled with sacks of collection boxes on the roof, in the boot and in the backseat. We got there, and I handed a box to the TANU Youth League volunteers on which I wrote the number of the box, and I wrote down who got it. He or she signed it, and then I said, I will come back here the day before I am leaving, and we will give you a receipt for your money. They go to their home area, sometimes many miles away. They would go off and collect and come back. Once I distributed the box, I got out in the car with the district or regional TANU secretary or whoever they gave me to visit a series of villages with village meetings they had set up. I would do this for each district and with the regional committees, and you know, I would address the meeting first, of course, with an interpreter. I had a sentence which I had worked out:

"Sorry, I can't speak Swahili, but I have only just come."

And then I would tell them about the college and why it was being established; that we needed money; that this was their college; how you got people to get there [apply]; how they would be selected; and what qualifications they had to have.

AT: Did they need formal education?

JW: No. They had to be able to read and write, and they had to know enough English to benefit from the course because there were no books and no tutors.

AT: How would they know English if they had not been to primary school?

JW: Well, they might have been a cook. Some people had been to primary school. Most people had been to primary school, probably for four years. They had the basics. Obviously, they had to be able to read and write. Some would have had to have acquired that knowledge. We did this again by organising essays. You had to write them on their own. You could not guarantee that, but we interviewed anybody who looked good on their essays. We had a hundred applications the first year. I went doing that [soliciting applications], but not in all the regions. I couldn't do it. But I did it in Lake Region. This was the whole of the eastern lake. I did it in southern highlands, which stretched all the way from Morogoro on down to Mbeya. I did it in Tabora region, and somehow Dodoma got in there too. Also, in Arusha and Moshi, some of the mountain but not much, mostly [the towns of] Arusha and Moshi, and Tanga and, of course, Dar es Salaam. I never got to the south at that point. I did when I was doing interviews with students later.

We got an enormous reception. I discovered one-cent pieces with a hole in the middle. I came across these strings of one-cent pieces. Sometimes I had to take the strings apart and drop them in one by one. Sometimes I got a 5 [cent pieces]. People really were very good. The advantage of a 10 cent was that I gave pieces of paper which I had on a pin and told them you could only get a piece of paper if you contributed at least 10 cents. But I think I put it in terms of a brick. I can't remember exactly what it was; certainly, it was something you had to do for 10 cents. We used to collect this money, you see. If the collectors were there, they would go and put it in their boxes. But if there weren't any collectors in that village, they would have to put it on a trestle table, if that is what we had or whatever it was that I was standing on or sitting on, or put it in my lap. I wasn't wearing slacks in those days. We collected all this money. We had some bags from the bank, and we put these coins in the bags. Wherever I slept, they were put under the bed; then we moved on. Wherever I was going, they went under the car seat, perfectly safe in those days, in a TANU car, absolutely safe. We would go on [to] however many places this was, it could be many places until we came to a town with a bank in it, and then we would go and put [deposit] it. It was tremendous.[82]

---

[82] In a written account of the formation of Kivukoni College, Wicken writes that "on the later safari to Southern Highlands, where there was no major peasant cash crop, an old lady said she had no money, so could she give an egg? It was auctioned immediately, and I remember the Asian merchant who had stopped to see what was going on, and paid the equivalent of 25 cents for it (in the market eggs were sold for less than one cent each). After that experience, we always asked for whatever they could give; very often the car became loaded with small tins of beans, groundnuts, or maize flour, or whatever else grew locally — including live chickens. The sheep we once received created a problem and much laughter! All the goods were taken to the next village meeting — for we had several a day — and sold on

AT: You raised enough to do what?

JW: We got £17,500 of one-cent pieces. What I remember are the one-cent pieces. I remember the rate of exchange was 20 shillings to the pound.

AT: What did you do with the money?

JW: Well, we had to pay for the price of the building. We had to furnish the building. We had to buy books. Before it was opened, we had internal self-government. We got some grants, but not really capital at all. We did it all with what we collected. We had £15,000 from the Karimjee Education Trust Fund.[83] We had £5,000 from TANU, £5,000 from the TFL treasury, and £5,000 from the co-ops together. Also, £5000 from the Ithna-Asheri community. We really had got an amount, £39,000 or something like that. We didn't have enough money to run it. We did everything on a shoestring. A lot of voluntary work went into it.

----

the college's behalf by the Youth League. "Kivukoni College, Dar es Salaam, Tanzania" by Joan E.Wicken (unpublished account).
[83] In the interview she said £15,000 but she indicated £30,000 in her unpublished written account, "Kivukoni College, Dar es Salaam, Tanzania" by Joan E.Wicken.

AT: What kind of people taught there?

JW: Colin Leys was the principal from Balliol College when it started. Most [principals] were interviewed by the principal of Ruskin College, Billy Hughes,[84] who came over about 2 or 3 years after independence after the college was opened to look at the college and make some suggestions of what we could do to improve it. It was called Kivukoni College.[85] Kivukoni means, as you know, at the crossing place. It was opened in July 1961 with 39 students, of whom three were women.

We had to fight to get women. We did not have many applications. One of the applications was from

---

[84] Billy Hughes (1914–1995) was a British Labour Party member of parliament from 1945–1950 and principal of Ruskin College from 1950–1979.

[85] Kivukoni College was inaugurated June 29, 1961. It was a college for all people, not for the elite. In 1971 it became the party Ideological College to spread and reinforce the ideology of TANU and be a source of ideas for the party. After the adoption of multipartyism in 1992, it became Kivukoni Academy of Social Sciences and in 2005 it was renamed the Mwalimu Nyerere Memorial Academy that provided degree programs mainly in the social sciences.

Julie Manning, who became a judge.[86] She was the first woman judge. There was no hostel, and the college was still being built. It wasn't a university, and they started off in the Lumumba St. building, which is the co-op building at the other end from TANU headquarters. Later it became the headquarters of the extramural department. The women actually lived in the Salvation Army camp, and I was officially their warden.[87]

AT: Can you tell me more about Julie Manning?

JW: I think her parents or grandparents, I don't know, were emigrés from South Africa and obviously there was some European ancestry at some point… Did you ever meet her? A tall, rather retiring, very dignified woman. Shy. She was the most outstanding of those first ones at the university. She was not at all

---

[86] Julie Manning was the first Tanzanian woman to study law at the University of East Africa. She drafted laws in the Attorney General's Chamber. She was appointed as a judge in the High Court of Tanzania in 1973, making her the first female African High Court judge in East Africa. Later she served as Minister of Justice from 1975 to 1983, making her one of the first two women in Tanzania's cabinet.

[87] Wicken lived in the Salvation Army camp for the duration of her time in Tanzania.

political. But remember, the first faculty to start was the law faculty. So, she was one of the first graduates.

AT: Who were some of the others?

JW: I can't remember. They had this hut immediately opposite mine, but I didn't, in fact, [see them] much. I got back late, and I was working late, so we didn't see much of each other. I would ask,

"Is everything alright?"

And they would reply, "Yes."

I didn't do anything useful there. But I was there if they wanted me. Well, some of the time. I mean, I was around.

AT: Were you with Kivukoni for two years?

JW: I wasn't there at all. I never did work in Kivukoni. I organised it. Set it up. Colin Leys came out, and he took over the sort of equipping of the college and getting the administrative staff and taking on people as cooks and cleaners.

AT: How long was he there then?

JW: He gave his notice before the college opened. I was so angry. He was there altogether for nearly a year, probably ten months or so. We didn't get on. I think he resented the fact that Kivukoni was identified with me. I had been travelling in the country. I had been meeting the National Executive [Committee of TANU]. People knew me. He came in, and people would come and ask me about the college, and I would ask him or suggest he would go and meet them.

One morning I was told that the NEC[88] was going to visit the college in the afternoon. OK, well, that is the way they worked. But Colin did not take kindly to that and just went off in the afternoon. So, of course, I had to take them around. But he resented that enormously. This was not his dignity. He should have been consulted and asked. He was a mistaken appointment. I mean, he did a good job in getting it organised and so on, but he did not like this. He went to Makerere [University]. Somehow, we got the idea that he had been in the government, and Ruskin recommended him. Of course, he was quite good academically. Still, he was quite right-wing and he could not get on with Africans, and his attitude was wrong. He was very resentful of the fact that Kivukoni was identified with me at that point. It was only a question of time, but he wasn't prepared for that. He obviously didn't expect it. There was also, of

---

88 National Executive Committee of TANU

course, Cran Pratt,[89] who was a friend of his. He came in shortly after as a principal at the University [of Dar es Salaam]. I think that he [Leys] also found that difficult because the university was obviously much more prestigious. But I was fantastically surprised to discover later that he was regarded as a Marxist. It took me a long time [to accept that]. I still do find it difficult to think of Colin as a Marxist.

So, the college was opened at the very end of July, but [it] had started before that and students did several things – songs and dances and skits about their colleagues and all the personalities, including Mwalimu, me, and Colin. We also had a Canadian, Griff Cunningham, who later became principal, the third one, not the second. When he got back [to Canada], he became a teacher at York University in Toronto. He does a lot with adult part-time students

---

[89] Cranford Pratt held academic appointments at McGill University and Makerere University (Uganda). He was a professor of political science at the University of Toronto for over four decades. In 1960, Pratt was appointed as the first Principal of the newly founded University of Dar es Salaam. For the next four years he oversaw both the construction of the campus as well as the appointment of new faculty.

as well as being a full-time university professor and has been there ever since.

Then we had Ethan Mayisela, who was from Swaziland [Eswatini].[90] I honestly can't remember how we came across him. I just can't remember, but anyway, he was on the staff. In the beginning, that was the academic staff. We had 39 students the first year, out of 400 applications, and everybody shortlisted was interviewed. Then we had this terrible jump. We were aiming for 30 students, but we had to push it up to 39. I wouldn't have got any women otherwise. None of the women had been heard from long after Kivukoni. One of them left early because she got pregnant.

We couldn't give them any money. They had quite a bit of land around at that time, and we had a shamba, and they grew some of their own food. The idea was that they would become self-reliant in food, or at least the basic foods, but they never did that. They had to clean their own rooms, but in the end, they didn't. Colin, probably rightly, gave up quite quickly on any idea that they would keep the common rooms

---

[90] Ethan Mayisela became the first governor of the Central Bank of Eswatini.

clean, corridors and so on. He got some cleaners and some cooks and again quite rightly so. The idea that they would cook for themselves, [that] wouldn't work. Then they had a secretary, a bookkeeper, a grasskeeper, and so on. We got a library; it was very basic, it had to be. It was basically simple economics. For some of them, English continued to be a problem when they had to read anything. They were very slow readers. Griff and Ethan, and Colin were supposed to be teaching. I think Colin found it difficult and frustrating to start at their level and to use their other experiences because, of course, they all had some. Many of them had been active in either the trade unions or the co-ops or TANU, and a couple of them in church groups. I think two or three had been doing voluntary adult education work and literacy, so they had varied experience, and they came from different parts of the country.

AT: What kinds of courses did they take?

JW: Well, it was basically a simple history of Tanganyika, economics (with Ethan), sociology, politics, the labour movement in Britain and elsewhere, with a particular emphasis on Britain because we didn't know much about what was going on elsewhere. Where possible, we taught about other African countries. We did have some other Africans.[91] Sam Nujoma[92] went to Kivukoni [to teach]. We had two other people; one was a chap from South Africa and another one from Uganda. We got a man from the Caribbean, don't ask me how, but we did. I think there were about four or five from other African countries.

AT: I thought of it much more as an ideological school? Did that change at some point?

JW: Yes, the party took it over [in 1971].

AT: I thought it was started by the party?

JW: No, it was started by the Education Trust, of which seven of its 13 members were TANU people, but it had its own separate governing body. The party took

---

[91] The first Tanzanian tutor was Daudi Mwakawago (1965–1970.) He also held the post of Vice Principal (1970), and of Principal (1971–1972, 1977–1980). He held several ministerial positions and served as ambassador to Italy and Permanent Representative to the Food and Agriculture Organization. He was also a member of Parliament (1970–1990, as well as the CCM Central Committee and National Executive Committee (1977–1992).

[92] Sam Nujoma served as the first president of Nujoma for three terms, from 1990 to 2005. He was the first president of the South West African People's Organization, which led the struggle for independence from South Africa from 1966 to 1989.

it over in the 1970s. They changed the governing body when they took it over. I was never on it. Colin was not happy that I might be on it, so I was not on it, but I knew what was going on. What I really resented, which I learned of, later on, [was that] he left a letter for his successor in which he told him to beware of me and how difficult I was and so on. I didn't ever understand why. He [the successor to Leys] was also unsuitable. He was an anthropologist. He thought in tribal terms and went around asking everybody what tribe they were. This was Arthur Scotney. He was the second principal after Leys. He had a three-year contract, but by mutual agreement, we ended it at two years.

AT: So, how long were you involved as secretary of the Education Trust?

JW: Theoretically, I still am the secretary of the Education Trust. Several times I urged that it be disbanded because nothing was happening.

AT: Why?

JW: Because it hadn't done anything in years. The last meeting of the trustees was in 1984. Theoretically, the Education Trust was going to do other work, and they did start setting up a college for women in Rugamba,

in Lady Chesham's[93] old place. She had already
sold it to a thing called the "Non-racial Education
Trust,"[which was] set up before independence and
before we had come on the scene. But St. Michael's and
St. George's School in Iringa were originally intended
to be the preparatory schools, public schools in the
British sense, non-racial, to get everybody together
and break down racial barriers, but along the lines
of a private school, boarding and like. But, in fact,
that school was never like that. At what point that
changed, I don't know, because it was already open
by the time I arrived. I only learned later what it had
been intended for. They had bought this piece of land
and certain buildings and had then built a college
for a preparatory school for the public school, again
English style, where you send your children away at

---

[93] Lady Marion Chesham (1903–1973) was a member of the
Tanganyika Legislative Council between 1958 and 1962. She
then went on to become a member of parliament until 1964.
She was aligned with TANU and was a close friend of Nyerere's.
Born in Philadelphia, United States, she became a Tanganyikan
citizen. She used her connections abroad to fund small scale
rural development and became the executive director of the
Community Development Trust Fund in 1961, holding this post
until 1971.

the age of eight or thereabouts to a boarding school to prepare them for entry to public school. But they had not finished building that, and it was agreed that they would close their trust down and give the college building their assets and their library. They didn't have a library to give, but very little money came with it. It was basically the buildings. It came to the Tanganyika Education Trust, and we were planning to start a college for women. Ours was the Tanganyika Education Trust. Theirs was the Non-Racial Education Trust, and they closed it down, and they gave us Rugambwa. Our idea was that we were going to finish building and equipping it as a college running short courses for women.

AT: Was Lady Chesham involved with the Education Trust?

JW: Not that I know of. Her husband died before independence, and I don't suppose she had much money. Any money he had in England probably went to someone else. He had been married before. It probably went to his son.

AT: She had some money.

JW: She was not without money, but she probably wanted to capitalise some of her critical assets.

Anyway, somehow they got this property from her, and we took it over.

Romantic Involvements

MLS: Did you have any romantic involvements? Did you think about raising a family?

JW: I didn't. I thought about it. I did, of course. I was never beautiful, but I had the freshness and enthusiasm of youth like everybody else. Yes, I had boyfriends. I think twice I got really serious, but in one case, the person was interested in me and engaged to someone else. We were boyfriend, girlfriend. But I went on leave and came back and found he was engaged to someone else next door. But yes, there was him, and there was another one whom I was very fond of at Ruskin College. That was quite a problem because he was a communist, and I saw it as a problem. Then we had the 1950 election in which the Labour Party lost some seats because a communist ran [split the votes], and [the Labour candidate] was defeated by a conservative by a small margin. I felt then, how could I survive sitting here with results like that with my husband wanting one [candidate] coming in [to win] and I wanted someone else to come in. I couldn't do it. So we parted. We had never gotten engaged or anything like that, but it was serious. Then there was somebody else with whom I did have an affair, but marriage was out of the question from his point of view.

MLS: Was he a Tanzanian?

JW: No. And I was certainly not [involved] with the president, Mwalimu. No. He knew about my other involvement and sympathised, but we never talked about it. I still think now it would have been a stupid thing to do [to marry the love interest].

WORKING WITH NYERERE

Being Hired (1960)

JW: At this time, after Kivukoni was opened, I was supposed to return. But, in fact, Mwalimu asked me to come to his office — he was then Prime Minister — and help him get ready for independence. This was just a few months before independence. "Well," I said, "I am tired. I must have a holiday. I must go home. People are expecting me." So they gave me my fare home and a return ticket. I went home for a month, I think. Then I came back and went into the Prime Minister's office as his personal assistant. I was interviewed. I mean, it was all arranged between Mwalimu and myself. But, of course, this was still the British civil service, so I was interviewed by Kim [Charles] Meek, who was then Permanent Secretary to the Prime Minister, the chief minister.[94] So he interviewed me about this job, and it was agreed that I would get the same pay as I got before: this mythical £850. At that time, I don't think that it should have been linked to someone else's pay, but I don't know what it was. Anyway, the point is that I got what I had been getting. They talked about an [additional] expatriate allowance. It didn't seem right. I didn't want an expatriate allowance. Just £850. I said you had forgotten one thing. I must have free medical attention. If I am living and working in England, I have a national health service. I want the same thing here. So that was agreed. Everything was agreed, and nothing was signed.

He said, "Fine, well, I'll see you [at] 7:30 am on Monday morning."

I said, "What?"

"I'll see you [at] 7:30 am in the morning."

"You won't!"

"What do you mean?"

---

[94] Charles "Kim" Meek served as Permanent Secretary in the office of the Chief Secretary and from 1960 to 1962 he served as Permanent Secretary to the Prime Minister (Nyerere) and Secretary to the Cabinet.

"I can't take a job that requires me to be there at 7:30 am in the morning. I can't do it!"

So, this sort of set him back a bit. I said,

"Not this one."

So, we agreed that I would work at 9 o'clock. I usually start work at 9:30 am.

As far as I was concerned, I was not going to take the job; it was as simple as that. I reckon I did just as much work as anyone else, and I stayed until 9 pm, but 7:30 am, no way! I did try.

I got two-year contracts over time, and I did get an increase over time. At one point, I was suggesting to Mwalimu that it was time I resigned and take some job in England. Well, we didn't get anywhere on that, but later I was querying if I should renew my contract. I [had renewed my contract] three times altogether, but suddenly [this time] I discovered I got two jumps on the [pay] scale. I said,

"That is not what *Ujamaa* was about."[95]

But anyway, I accepted. I went on. As I say, I was still there.

---

[95] *Ujamaa* was Tanzania's socialist policy as formulated by Nyerere. It was based on the idea of the nation as family and egalitarianism.

Speechwriter for Nyerere (1961–1985)

AT: What were your duties working with Nyerere?

JW: I did just what he wanted me to do from beginning to end.

AT: What was that? What did you do?

JW: Drafting speeches. But I do want to stress, for Mwalimu, it was drafting speeches. At the beginning, we would talk about it for some time, for example, his independence speeches. This is the sort of thing I was taken on for. The civil service can do a civil service speech. They couldn't do a political speech, and I could do something towards that, but at that stage, I wasn't, of course, sufficiently familiar with all the details. I never did draft anything in Swahili because he wouldn't accept it. Paul Sozigwa[96] did the translation [into Swahili].

What used to happen was that if it was to be given in Swahili, I would do a draft in English. If the general outline was right and I had got things basically right,

---

[96] Paul Sozigwa was press secretary to President Nyerere from 1967 until 1985. Prior to that post, he had been a journalist and had served as Permanent Secretary to the Ministry of Information and Tourism. He had also served on the TANU Central Committee.

Mwalimu would say: "I want more emphasis on this bit or on that," or [he would] put a cross through something or put a note in, "Add this," and I would add something, and then that would be redone and given to him. Usually, at that point, that would be the end of the alterations he would make in English. Then, he would make a few more, and I would put it on my copy and Paul would take it over and do a translation into Swahili, and that would go to Mwalimu, and Mwalimu would then edit the Swahili version. I was always chasing behind, trying to keep my English compatible with what he had changed [in the Swahili version]. Which is why you always got Mwalimu's speeches in two copies, in Swahili and English, almost simultaneous, because I was chasing every draft.

Mwalimu always had long drafts. He had tremendous input. That is why in the early days, we used to talk about all the speeches a lot, what he wanted to say and what the background was. Because over time, you accumulate knowledge. Sometimes later, when time was pressing, Mwalimu would just say, "I want a talk on the Middle East" or something. I am thinking of 1967 when he was very much against Israel's attack on Egypt and Syria, and he held so many press conferences and speeches on it. Finally, I said to him:

"Not another one!"

"Do you think I've made too many?" he asked.

I replied, "Yes!" particularly because I didn't like the subject too much.

AT: Did he ad-lib a lot?

JW: Mostly, he read it. In the beginning, he didn't ad-lib because he would lose it [his train of thought] until he got used to the idea. He would nearly always put in the odd sentence or phrase or repeat something in the written speech, but generally, he stuck to it. He did more ad-libbing in his Swahili speeches.

AT: I recall people quoting things he had said, they were Swahili proverbs, and I am sure they didn't come from you.

JW: What I would do is say, in a case like that, "The English proverb I am thinking of is … have you got the Tanzanian equivalent?" Sometimes he would put them in himself.

AT: I see. Some Swahili speeches sounded like they came in the moment.

JW: Well, that could happen in Swahili. If he was doing a mass meeting, he often wouldn't have a draft at all.

If he was going to Jangwani, very rarely did he use a
speech. In that case, he would do a lot of ad-libbing
and put in jokes. Only if it was some international
thing, he was talking about, and he wanted to make
sure that the British or Americans or Germans or
whatever got it right. When he travelled abroad, he
almost always tried to have a prepared speech. When
he spoke to an international audience or gave a major
lecture, like to the FAO,[97] the [Ndugu memorial
speech] in 1963, which was one of his big ones, and
the Hammerskjöld Memorial lecture in 1964, that
was in Dar es Salaam, the week of the mutiny. It was
very funny. We had been working on that for a long
time. It is one that I think is a good one. Probably my
favourite is the FAO one in 1963; it is in *Freedom and
Unity*.[98] So is the Hammerskjöld Memorial lecture.

---

[97] Food and Agriculture Organization
[98] Julius K. Nyerere, *Freedom and Unity—Uhuru na Umoja: A
Selection from Writings and Speeches, 1952–65*. London, Nairobi,
Dar es Salaam, Ibadan: Oxford University Press. 1967.

Personal Assistant to Nyerere (1961–1999)

AT: You said you were his assistant until 1984?

JW: No, I stayed on because he asked me to come back. First, to come back when he was still chairman of the party. By that time, the South Commission had started. I had definitely given my notice then, and he had accepted it. I had undertaken to go back to Somerville, where I had been offered a visiting fellow or something, where I was going to write up these notes. But he said that this had been arranged before he came to his final conclusion about me and about the South Commission.

When he started talking about me doing something, I said,

"You do realise I won't be here."

He replied, "What do you mean you won't be here?"

I said, "You know, we agreed that I was leaving."

"You can't do that. You pushed me into this [the South Commission]."

I replied, "I didn't push you into it. All I did was pass along messages."

He said, "You did more than that. You can't leave me now. You started me on this. You have got to stay until it is finished."

Well then, after that, there was [I worked with him at] the South Commission.[99]

AT: Obviously, there was something that worked in your relationship. He must have trusted you an awful lot.

JW: He could say things to me and know it wouldn't go anywhere else. This is why [my notes] are going to be embargoed.[100] Because he didn't often talk about other people as people, basically, it was much more about the issues. But he wasn't guarding what he said. It is disgusting how little I have got. My memory is no good, although I do remember odd things. Sometimes my memory is quite different from my notes, I noticed. At least it is different in emphasis. But we [Nyerere and I] could talk about anything.

---

[99] The South Commission (1987–90) was created by Julius Nyerere. It was formed to strengthen cooperation between countries in the global South. It gave rise to the South Centre, which is based in Geneva, Switzerland. The South Centre is an independent intergovernmental think-tank of developing countries whose goal is to analyse development problems of countries in the South and share experiences and find common solutions.

[100] When I interviewed Wicken, she was in the process of typing up her notes and they were to be sealed in the Bodleian archives, Oxford University, for thirty years.

I would argue with him, which not many people would.

Amir Jamal[101] was able to argue with Mwalimu, and that was something he valued very much. Mwalimu liked being argued with. But he didn't like being challenged. I was not challenging him, but neither was Amir. I mean, I didn't challenge him in his basic approach. I was a socialist before I ever came to him, so was Amir. Amir was a Fabian. He did a lot of reading. I thought the world of Amir, and so did Mwalimu.

We [Nyerere and I] fitted well together. I could argue with him—and I was nearer in age [to Nyerere], which is important— in a way that the youngsters found difficult. I could argue with him on age alone and because I had known him before he had any position. He was already [the] leader of the [party] when I knew him. We got along well. Our ideas on the basics were very similar.

---

[101] Amir Jamal (1922–1995) served as a Minister of Finance for 12 years. He held numerous other government portfolios, including Minister for Commerce and Industries. He was elected to the Legislative Council in 1958. He joined TANU in 1962. He represented Morogoro in the parliament from 1960 to 1985.

AT: How would you characterise your relationship with him? Was he a friend? Was he a confidant?

JW: He never talked to me about security matters. At one point, we used to get those letters from Amnesty [International], and I took to answering some of these to put the government's case. Then, of course, they would write back. My letter was too nice and reasonable, arguing the case. I sent copies to the Minister of Home Affairs. I would normally have done that. Anyway, he [the Minister] went to Mwalimu and told me to stop, so I did. He spoke to Mwalimu, and Mwalimu told me to stop. They did what they wanted. My instruction was clear. I just carried it out.

AT: Were you a confidant on personal matters? Did he talk to you about his family, for example?

JW: Rarely. Sometimes he would bemoan the fact that he was a very bad father. He had taken no part in the upbringing of his children. But, of course, he was away, and it all fell on his wife.[102] She broke under the strain, really. So that got dragged up. They never

---

[102] Maria Nyerere married Julius Nyerere in 1953 and they had seven children, Maria, John, Anna, Rosemary, Makongoro, Madaraka, Andrew and Maggie.

went hungry, but sometimes before independence, before he had any official position, they had no money coming in. She had seven children before independence.

He was very much a member of [his extended] family and the most prosperous member of the family. Nobody else got his kind of salary, as lousy as it was in African terms.

AT: He probably had enormous demands from his family.[103]

JW: Yes, from his extended family. In the late 1980s, there was a family gathering of all the generations for some reason in Butiama, and there were 300 people there all connected through brothers. Remember, there were 26 children by his father, and they all got married, they all had children. I said to Mwalimu once, do you know how many grandchildren you have got, and he said, "I haven't a clue."

AT: To go back to my earlier question: Were you a confidant, a friend to Nyerere?

---

[103] According to Paul Bjerk, Bhoke Munaka and later Joseph Butiku handled many of his family responsibilities (Personal communication May 11, 2021).

JW: I was mostly a personal assistant. But simply because I could do that job in a particular way and [because] we were friends of long-standing.

AT: And because you were discreet?

JW: I guess he found that out. He would not have known that from the beginning, would he? That is not the important thing.

AT: What do you think was your contribution to Tanzania?

JW: I want to get off [talking about] me.

AT: Well, just answer this, what do you think you contributed?

JW: I made Mwalimu's job a little bit easier on the margins. I was helpful to him more than anything else. I hope that in the course of doing that, I contributed to the development of socialism in Tanzania. I was recruited to that job because I was a socialist, a socialist working in adult education first.

MLS: Were you ever a Marxist?

JW: I was never a Marxist. I haven't read Marx. I still haven't read Marx.

AT: Were you a Fabian?

JW: Only in the sense that I knew some of them and had close contact with them. But I was never even a member [of the Fabian Society]. But we were closely associated and knew each other; sometimes, if they were organising a meeting, we would cooperate and vice versa.

When the Arusha Declaration came out, I knew nothing about it at all. I did get the job later of translating it into English, but that was after it was already public. He checked it over. There was still one sentence I didn't get right. It talked about communications; I took it to mean railways and roads. In fact, it had both meanings [infrastructure for transportation and media]. When they nationalised two major newspapers, this was used in support of that, which I had not realised. The first translation was corrected in the second translation to make it clear that it meant both kinds of communications. That was the only thing that had slipped by Mwalimu.

AT: Are there any policies that you think you might have helped influence, or was it all him?

JW: It was him. I believed that I helped him to express himself, particularly in writing. Because I argued with him, he had to sometimes think how to meet an objection. Now, how often, if at all, this ever changed his position or view on a particular issue, I don't know. Certainly not on the basic principles. But we were at one on those. I couldn't have done anything on my own. I was a stranger to him. Mwalimu was a Tanzanian, and any Tanzanian would know the country better than I do.

Even in my early days, it seemed to me that Tanzanians knew Tanzania. I might know other things, but they knew Tanzania and what would work there. I used to get horrified at the way some people [foreigners] thought they had all the answers. I didn't ever feel that, but I would argue from my own background. I would talk, he would listen. I have no idea why. Sometimes we would discuss things, and I knew the general thrust of what he was thinking of doing. Sometimes he would develop it. Sometimes he didn't. You know we had been talking about these things as friends do, but he had been talking to lots of other people.

I don't think I was an influence. I was a donkey at work.

AT: A sounding board perhaps is a better way of describing it.

JW: Yes, a sounding board.

AT: Were you ever tempted to leave?

JW: No. I figured if I really disagreed with anything, then it was my job to go. I never went.

AT: Any regrets?

JW: You know, sometimes, when life is hard, and you get lonely, you say, "What the hell am I doing here?" But I mean, that is there in any job. I met a lot of leaders. I had a list of four, including Mwalimu, whom I thought were in a class of their own: Olaf Palme, [Fidel] Castro, and Chou Enlai.

AT: Not Mandela?

JW: No, I had never met him. This goes way back. I had met a lot of people. I met Mengistu.[104] I remember sitting, taking notes at a meeting and at dinner. Mengistu had a very attractive personality, and I believe this is genuine. He was also a murderer. And I was sitting there saying [to myself], "That man is a murderer, but he is very good." I felt he wasn't a murderer for the sake of murdering or even for the sake of his own power. He was committed 100 per cent plus to the unity of Ethiopia. He said, "If I don't fight this and win, Ethiopia will split up," which, of course, it did. The system they have there now, they are still holding together. It might be the right one except for Eritrea, which was probably inevitable

---

[104] Mengistu Haile Mariam was president of Ethiopia from 1977 to 1991.

by that time. But he was highly intelligent, able to argue with Mwalimu and anybody else, obviously not with me; I was not in that position. But he was a murderer, no question about it. And I would sit there thinking, "There is a murderer." But I respected the fact that he wasn't doing it for personal reasons. I am not aware, I have no way of really knowing if he was personally corrupt, but I doubt it. I doubt if he went to Zimbabwe[105] with anything much in the way of personal money. Obviously, he used a government plane to get out. I can excuse something like that, but it doesn't mean I liked it or I approved of it because I don't think that is the way of solving problems.

Mwalimu obviously didn't do it that way. Mwalimu did not have the same inheritance, the same difficulties. There were other factors: Mwalimu, by inclination, was the sort of person who taught and sat under a tree and argued until you agreed. That was his instinct and his nature. But there were advantages. The Swahili language, even before TANU, among men, in particular, was very widespread. I once asked Mwalimu how many times during the independence

---

[105] Mengistu went into exile in 1991, where he remains. An Ethiopian court found him guilty of genocide in absentia.

struggle, from the formation of TANU onward, did he have to get an interpreter. He said four times. Now how many hundreds of meetings did he have? Which other leader, except for the Somalis, could have done that? No other country in Africa could do that. Look at Zambia. Even to the end, Ken Kaunda had to have interpreters in many parts of Zambia, even with the Copperbelt there.

Working with Rashidi Kawawa (1962)

AT: What years were you with Kawawa?

JW: I was [a] personal assistant helping him with speeches.

AT: Which years?

JW: When Mwalimu resigned from being president on January 26, 1962, until he came back as president [in December of 1962]. For all that period, Rashidi was prime minister, and Mwalimu just told me to work for him. I doubt Rashidi was given any choice in the matter either. But both of us sort of muddled through. If Mwalimu says so, you do it [laughter]. Nyerere was still [the] leader of the party—he was very much involved. He wasn't talking to me much then because I was working for Rashidi anyway. I lost contact with Nyerere at that time.

Kawawa was prime minister for a while, and then he was dropped. It didn't matter for Rashidi. What Mwalimu wanted him to do, he did it. We weren't close, but I got on well with Rashidi. I worked for him during that gap [January to December 1962]. It was quite difficult for both of us I think when I would talk to him to get some guidance from him. I could only do what he asked me to do [and this was limited]. But that was my job, but it was not easy.

AT: It sounds like he was loyal and did his job well, but he was not a sounding board for Mwalimu.

JW: No. I don't think he would have been. I am sure Mwalimu talked with him, but no, he did not have the background or education, and it wasn't his instinct. I think his father was a hunter. That is where he got his discipline. He never joined the army. He came up through the trade unions, and he was head of the trade unions. When he became second vice president instead of first vice president, he said,

"Mwalimu wants me to do it. It doesn't matter what Mwalimu wants me to do; I'll do it. If he wants me to black [polish] his shoes, I'll do it."

He meant it. He was very genuine.

He had limitations, and he always did. But on loyalty and hard work and commitment, no second. I am not saying as far as loyalty; he was the only one. I mean, Amir Jamal and many others were loyal, but unlike with Rashidi, there was no question of Amir ever becoming president or vice president.[106] We have to face realities in life, namely the anti-Asian prejudice. You would get a tirade against the Asians. And I would say,

"You know, you are just talking about a whole group of people, regardless. You know you are including Amir Jamal."

And then they would say, "Oh no, he is different." There was no way he was going to be prime minister.

AT: Wasn't Kawawa behind the Operation Maduka disaster?[107]

---

[106] Jamal was born to Gujarati parents of Indian descent and in the Tanzanian context, this would have precluded him from becoming president, even though theoretically it would have been possible.

[107] Operation Maduka was a shortlived 1976 campaign to put all shops under government control. It had its heaviest impact on Asian and Arab shop owners, since at this time only about 30 percent of Dar es Salaam's shops were owned by Africans.

JW: Yes, that was Rashidi. Like I said, [it was] not because he intended to cause problems. The idea was to encourage co-ops. But Rashidi's idea of encouraging co-ops was to close down everything [laughter]. So that is just the sort of thing I mean, that he was trying to carry out Mwalimu's policy. Mwalimu was not dealing with details all the time. He was much more the sort of strategic man.

AT: I was being followed by a government spy (*shushushu*) when I was doing my study of informal economy in the mid-1980s. I feel like I owe Kawawa my sanity while I was in Tanzania. I went to him to complain and to get them to call off the spy, and the next day she was gone. I think the spying has eased up, especially around hotels and downtown areas.

JW: Security was one of the things Mwalimu did not deal with [as he did not deal with] details. And certainly, sometimes, that was rough. I remember someone writing an anonymous letter making these allegations. This was a terrible case. Mwalimu was very upset by this. He did not know what to do. There was nothing, no date on the letter, and there was no way to get down to when these things were said to have occurred. We could not get down to this, when and where. We worried about it for a week. I said, "Can't you look to see who was on duty at the time?" I somehow assumed that the dates were there. So he got up immediately and dashed off to look at the letter again, and there were no dates. He said, "How could my security have done things like this?" And I don't think many of them would, but there were allegations like this. It may well have happened, but there was nothing we could do about it because there was no address, no signature. But you know security around the world is like that. They have their likes and dislikes.

People do get the idea they were followed. I know Mwalimu had various security reports on me. I was never conscious of being followed. But he had got these at least on several occasions. I don't know what they said or what they alleged. But I was very careful, and it seemed to me that I was in a very vulnerable position and in a position where people concerned with security should be.

Differences with Nyerere

AT: Was there any time that you disagreed with him when you did not like what he was doing or saying? After 40 years, you might have had some differences?

JW: I was very upset by the breaking up of the Ruvuma Development Association[108] and the pushing out of Ralph Ibbott.

AT: The RDA seemed very much like what Nyerere wanted anyway, so it was curious …

JW: It was, it was. I think that the real problem was that the villagers had understood the basics [of Nyerere's ujamaa policy] and were acting out the basics. What they didn't have, which is too much to ask, was the sort of tact to be able to understand the power positions. They expected the [TANU leaders] to be also socialist, and they weren't.

---

[108] Ruvuma Development Association (RDA) was established by villagers in the early 1960s as an collective self-help village and initially it was lauded by Nyerere. It was started by Ntimbanjayo Millinga, a leader of a local branch of the TANU Youth League and a British surveyor, Ralph Ibbott. It was strongly opposed by the party leadership, especially those at the mid-level, who felt threatened by the RDA and in 1969 the TANU Central Committee voted to shut it down.

There was a seminar. Again, Mwalimu did like their ideas. He organised a seminar on socialism and got Ralph Ibbot and John Ntimbanjayo Millinga, who later became an Area Commissioner and one or two others from there [RDA], to come and lead this [seminar] at Kivukoni. All the members of the NEC and the cabinet were to attend.[109] You see, these [RDA] people essentially said in so many words that the only socialists in this country were us in the Ruvuma Development Association and Mwalimu. Well, that was quite a challenge, wasn't it? It was not taken kindly. It went over very badly, and after that, it was simply a question of time. I don't know what the trigger was. Ralph Ibbot was thrown out of Tanzania for all the wrong reasons.

AT: Why was he thrown out?

JW: We were away on safari when it happened, but he must have known about it. Mwalimu backed it [his expulsion] when he got back. He defended it [the closing down of the RDA]. We understood that we didn't agree on that. I really wasn't there when it happened, and I don't know what the official reason was. Basically, they became too ambitious and very

---

109 This was a meeting of the Central Committee, not the NEC.

socialist. They were operating as socialists, but in so
doing, they were challenging the reluctance of some
members of the National Executive [Committee].[110]
But they really operated as a cooperative. When
visitors came, they expected them to join them in the
fields. They received them in a happy, friendly way;
everybody was always well received.[111]

AT: What other differences did you have with
Mwalimu?

JW: I was very worried about the one-party state in
the beginning. It got less so. It seems to me that it

---

[110] The National Executive Committee — referred to by Wicken
as "the National Executive", and by many others as NEC — was
the leading body in TANU and later Chama Cha Mapinduzi.

[111] In a personal communication with Leander Schneider,
Wicken had also suggested that external support for the RDA
may have also led to its disbanding of the RDA, given the history
of the suspicion of foreign interference in Tanzania. She wrote in
2002: "The influx of people from Europe and America was one
of the background elements which indirectly led to the killing of
the RDA ... In addition to Ralph [Ibbott] ... they did get more
British, and then some Americans — leading members of NATO
alongside Portugal, and being apparently sympathetic to it...
Anyway, the suspicions were there then" (Leander Schneider,
"Considering Tanzanian-Style Rural Socialism: One More
time?") http://www.arts.yorku.african_liberation/conference_
papers/Schneider_print.html Accessed October 31, 2005.

worked in Tanzania's circumstances. It was more
democratic than the multiparty system is now. TANU
was really a thoroughly democratic institution, and I
still believe it was more democratic than what we've
got now, but, of course, TANU did become corrupted,
more than corrupt. Corrupted in the sense of power
and not listening to people and being assured that
if you are secretary of the village or secretary of the
district, then you were the boss. You know that kind
of attitude, which hadn't been there in the beginning.

AT: How do you maintain an institution as democratic
and open without some challenge from somewhere,
which is what a multiparty system might provide?

JW: I think what I was expecting, naively perhaps,
was that the force of the people standing up for
themselves and their own rights would, in fact,
provide that. They would be checking up on their
leaders, secretaries, their own chairman. They were
electing their own chairman, of course, and they
would argue their points of view. I don't know how
and why they stopped being active. Maybe I was
asking too much to think that the enthusiasm of
the independence fight would continue, particularly
when leaders became power-drunk and when things
got tough economically. That gave power to people,

but many people would start standing up for a leader instead of checking the leader. Somebody had to be given the power to allocate a license or sugar in the village.

AT: Do you think it was more open after independence?

JW: Oh, yes, it was.

AT: What was the turning point?

JW: It was gradual. I do know that if there was a turning point, it was when TANU became CCM.

TURNING POINTS

The Zanzibar Revolution

AT: What is your interpretation of the events surrounding the Zanzibar Revolution?

JW: First, it took place in the context of the attempt to set up a Federation of East Africa, which is what Mwalimu was really after. If you remember, in 1963, the three leaders, Obote, Kenyatta[112] and Mwalimu, agreed to set up a Federation of East Africa after the independence of Kenya, which was the last one to become independent.[113] But anyway, they were

---

[112] Milton Obote was president of Uganda at the time. He had been prime minister (1962–1966) and president (1966–1971 and 1980–1985). Jomo Kenyatta was prime minister (1963–1964) and president of Kenya (1964–1978).
[113] Tanzania became independent in 1961, Uganda in 1962 and Kenya in 1963.

not going to do it under the British. There was a declaration that they were going to do this after independence. Mwalimu pushed that idea, persuaded them, got that agreement, and he, on his part, certainly was absolutely sincere. Kenyatta later said that this was utterly a ruse to get the British to [speed up efforts to] bring forward independence for Kenya. That was never true for Mwalimu. He had argued in 1960 or 1961; I can't remember at which meeting, where Mwalimu offered to delay the independence of Tanganyika so that the three countries could [form a federation], arguing that if they all got independence separately, it would be much more difficult to get the federation. That was why he was so pleased to get this agreement in 1963. We were already independent, but Kenya wasn't. Obote said they should all join in on the declaration. It was the intention. Mwalimu was absolutely dead set on it; there was no manoeuvring; that was what he wanted.

Those discussions went on. I remember a discussion in Dar es Salaam, and Kenya was represented by Tom Mboya, who was very keen on the idea. It was thought, [indeed] that one of the reasons for Kenya's rejection may have been his advocacy of it. But by late 1963, early 1964, Obote had said he could not go ahead now because of his problems with [the Buganda king], the Kabaka. He couldn't have a federation within the federation. And that was the way he was going to have to do it in Uganda. But the other two should go ahead, and they would be a sort of affiliate, or something, some sort of association, but they couldn't join for the time being.

Then Mwalimu said to Kenyatta, let us go ahead, and you be president. This was all done privately. Kenyatta, I don't know if he actually refused. I wasn't there. It is obvious this meeting was very private between the two. Whether he actually refused and said no or whether he just sort of pushed it aside, but anyway, he didn't want it. Of course, there were certain people, and, of course, Njonjo,[114] the leading opponent always, although we had not had the Arusha Declaration by then, but Tanzania was at least still officially socialist, which certainly Njonjo wasn't, and he wasn't the only one.

Kenyatta was worried about the Kikuyu, and he felt that this was, in part, an attempt to get him away from

---

[114] Sir Charles Njonjo (1920–) was the former Attorney General of Kenya (1963–1979), Minister of Constitutional Affairs (1980–1983) and Minister of Justice (1978–1982). In 1998 he was appointed chairman of the Kenya Wildlife Service.

Kenya. How much of this is interpretation, I can't remember. I wasn't there for that meeting anyway. Maybe [Kenyatta thought] it was part of a manoeuvre by Tom Mboya to get him away so Tom could take over in Kenya. That certainly was not the case. Tom was as honest as Mwalimu was. But anyway, in other words, Obote said,

"You go ahead without me."

[Nyerere] urged Kenyatta, "Let's go ahead."

Kenyatta said, "No."

There was another element in East Africa, which at that time, in 1963, of course, [that was] Zanzibar was not independent either. After the revolution [in January 1964], Mwalimu then said to Karume,[115]

"I've said to Kenyatta this, he doesn't want to [go ahead with the federation]; I am now saying it to you, do you want to go ahead?"

Karume said, "Yes."

They went ahead. That is how it [the union] started. It came up in that context.

---

[115] Abeid Karume was the first president of Zanzibar after the overthrow of the Omani Sultan of Zanzibar in 1964. After the United Republic of Tanzania was established in 1964, Karume became the Vice President of Tanzania. He served in these capacities until 1972, when he was succeeded by Aboud Jumbe.

But it also made sense, of course, geographically. The revolution made even more sense because it involved tribal politics [between Arabs and Africans in Zanzibar] and the division of Germany.[116] All this stuff had already come into play. Then the revolution was on 3 January 1964, and the mutiny was nine months later. [During the revolution in Zanzibar] Nyerere was concerned to stop the bloodshed very quickly. You had some Tanganyikans from the mainland police over there very early on.

The West had already written Zanzibar off as being anti-sultan; of course, that was the British policy, and they had decided that it was communist. What I knew of Karume or knew of his policies, he hadn't the slightest perception of either communism or capitalism. It was basically that he was president. He had been a seaman. But the East Germans and the Russians had come in and said, we are your friends; we will help you. Of course, he said, "Yes." So, there we were, getting West Germans on the mainland and East Germans on Zanzibar. We could become

---

[116] The role of East Germany in Zanzibar and West Germany in the mainland in the context of the Cold War and East-West rivalry.

very deeply involved in Cold War politics, so it made sense for us to try and establish a single sort of policy over the whole area, a single sovereignty. Mwalimu was very conscious, perhaps overly conscious, of the fact that because of its difference in size, Tanganyika would be said to be occupying Zanzibar. That is why you get this peculiar leadership arrangement because he was to try to balance it so that the two nations would be more equal.

The actual constitution, which now is funny to look at, has this idea of having a government in Zanzibar as well as being part of the union government. It was, of course, copied from the USA. You were uniting two separate sovereignties. You had to have one representative in the UN instead of two. Somebody had to withdraw one. It was tricky, and, of course, Mwalimu was supersensitive on this.

I don't think he has ever regretted the merger at all. The fact [was] that it gave him a lot of headaches, there is no question of that because of the constitution that he and Karume [came up with]. It was probably Roland Brown who really did the work [on the constitution]. The Zanzibaris had a lawyer who represented them in the negotiations, but Roland would certainly have been the most senior and more knowledgeable. Mwalimu's position really was to give the Zanzibaris what they wanted to get it [the union] going.

The 1964 Mutiny

AT: Tell me about the mutiny. How did you experience it?

JW: The mutiny took place on a Sunday night, Monday morning. Nyerere had been scheduled to give this Hammerskjöld Memorial Lecture on a Thursday. I thought it [the draft we worked on that Sunday night] would be more or less the final one. I can't remember how many times he came back with that because a major speech like that he would really work on. He did a lot on it, if only throwing it back with a few words changed. Remember, at that time, we didn't have word processors.

AT: You had to retype the whole thing?

JW: Yes. He reappeared on the scene on the Wednesday. There was a cabinet meeting. I cornered him afterwards, and I queried,

"What are you going to do about tomorrow [finalising the draft Hammarskjöld speech]?"

He said to me, "That is a good idea; yes, I will do it."

"But what about the draft? I gave it to you last week for further redrafting."

"Prepare it for delivery."

He then went off. I mean, he had other things on his mind that week. He came and delivered that speech. I don't know how. He was so apathetic.

The speech was basically about the idea that [there is] no point in talking about [the] rule of law if you don't have some authority. You must have an authority, a constitutional democratic authority, as far as possible. You must have an authority to keep the society going, to keep the peace.

So, of course, right in the middle of the mutiny, this is between the mutiny and the time the British are called in, we go there [to give the speech], and we have all been sweating blood, one way or another, Mwalimu, in particular.[117] I just go there, and sort of follow him. I tried to follow what he was actually saying and make notes where he changed it, just for the record. So I know exactly what he did say. Sometimes, like you say, he went off [script], but this really didn't arise very much. Many of his Swahili speeches were

---

[117] Speech in honour of Dag Hammarskjöld, January 24, 1964.

impromptu, as distinct from Mwinyi,[118] who never gave an impromptu speech at all. But anyway, I remember Mwalimu got tremendous applause when he arrived there before we even started. It was a lively audience of diplomats and academics. It was that sort of audience because it was that sort of occasion. His speech went well. He delivered it well, as though he had no other troubles at all. Then one woman, an American woman — who she was, I had no idea, and she didn't know me from Adam—said,

"It is marvellous how in the middle of this time, he has had a chance to prepare that speech in the last two days." [Laughter]

The subject was on authority.

AT: How did you feel at that time? Were you afraid? Was it a nerve-wracking time?

JW: Oh yes. It was the only time he did disappear.[119] There were people killed. It was slipping badly out of

---

[118] Ali Hassan Mwinyi (born 8 May 1925–) was the second president of the United Republic of Tanzania, from 1985 to 1995, following Nyerere. Prior to this, he had served as Interior Minister and Vice President. He was also chairman of CCM from 1990 to 1996.

[119] The Tanganyikan Army, known as the Tanganyikan Rifles, engaged in an attempted coup on January 20, 1964. The coup was said to be over the amount of their pay and the fact that British

control before Mwalimu finally gave in and agreed to the British offer [to send troops to quell the attempted coup]. The Kenyans and the Ugandans had both done it already. They had their mutiny after us, close on, within hours or days, and they called the British in immediately. Mwalimu was trying to avoid that. The one thing he really hated and felt humiliated by was having to do that. He really hated that. But the thing [attempted coup] was on the Monday night. When he came back to the office, he was trying various things to sort of reestablish control gently and delicately. His real test to the army was instructing that they should

....

officers were still in command after independence. The two battalions of 1,700 soldiers dismissed their British officers, even though this privilege belongs to the president. The troops seized the capital city of Dar es Salaam in events that led to 17 dead and 100 injured. Mobs were terrorising the city's Indian and Arab quarters, plundering shops, smashing windows and wrecking cars. Nyerere was not heard from for two days, until he called for calm in a national broadcast, saying, "My hope is that we shall never see such a disgrace repeated in Tanganyika" ("Tanganyika Leader Assails Mutiny and Asks for Calm," *New York Times*, January 21, 1964, https://www.nytimes.com/1964/01/22/archives/tanganyika-leader-assails-mutiny-and-asks-for-calm.html) By January 25, the mutiny had been suppressed by British troops, called in by President Nyerere.

all take off their combat uniforms and wear the number one dress or number two dress or whatever it was called. He gave that instruction, and it didn't happen. Then he realised he didn't have control of the army.

In my view, it started with genuine anger and dissatisfaction with the continuation of the British officers. This is what they did. They rounded all of them [the British officers] up and put them all on a plane. They commandeered whatever plane was there. But it is after that [when] they came demanding to see Mwalimu. When armies come to the president with guns, you don't let them do it, and so in the meantime, he had been got out [hidden]. I don't know where he went. I never asked, and I was never told. It wasn't my business. On Wednesday, he was back, and it was on the Friday evening [that] he finally gave way, and he decided to call in the British. I knew something was happening, but I didn't know what was happening.

At that time, we had an official personal secretary, a sort of typist, although [Mwalimu] never dictated anything — Mrs Wilson — you must have heard of her. You have probably been told she was his landlady [in Edinburgh], which she never was. She was the widow of a missionary medical doctor in Angola.

She had come out to Angola. I don't know whether he [her husband] died there or after they went back. She was living in Edinburgh working as a secretary, but she had a son at university. Somehow Mwalimu met the son, and he became a friend of the family. He would sometimes spend weekends with the family, and she, in a sense, mothered him. He became very fond of her, and she became fond of him. He invited her out for the independence celebrations and invited her out again for the republic celebrations. He then asked her to stay on as a personal secretary. She was living in the State House.

At [the time of] the mutiny when Nyerere disappeared, Maria [wife of Nyerere] arranged for Mrs Wilson to go out. She went to stay with the matron of Ocean Road Hospital, but she came back, I think, on Thursday night. On Friday, late afternoon, I was going up to see her, because she was back in the flat and Mwalimu saw me and said:

"What are you doing here?"

"I am going up to see Mrs Wilson," I replied.

"Where is she?" he demanded.

"She is upstairs," I replied.

He shouted, "Get her out!"

"When?"

"Now."

And then he went off. So, I just went up to Mrs Wilson and said,

"I think we had better move."

So, she went back to Matron's hospital. That was the night he called the British in. I guess Mwalimu was nervous. He didn't disappear, but he didn't want her around. I mean, she was an old woman even then. She died not too long after that. She went back to Scotland. He invited her out again later, and she came as a visitor. She was with him in Butiama. Mwalimu, in a sense, looked after her. She was a beautiful secretary, the best secretary anyone could ever have. Never made a mistake, ever. But she was an old woman. I can't think how old she would have been then. She would have been well into her sixties. People did not know about her; she never appeared anywhere.

AT: When other things were being Africanised, didn't people ever say anything about her presence in the State House or your working for Nyerere?

JW: They probably did to Mwalimu, but he certainly didn't tell me about it. I was told that this was raised in the NEC [TANU's National Executive Committee]

on one occasion.[120] There is always somebody who tells these things. I don't know [exactly] what he said, but he [may have] said to them, "I need her," "I want her," or something like that. When Mwalimu said that, they accepted it. You know, gradually, I think they began to realise I was harmless. Of course, I was known through Kivukoni.

Formation of Chama Cha Mapinduzi

AT: You mentioned earlier a turning point in support for the party. Can you elaborate?

JW: I think it was gradual. I think there was a turning point when TANU became CCM [Chama Cha Mapinduzi].[121]

AT: Why?

JW: If there was a turning point at all, it was at that point, and I think it certainly got worse very quickly.

---

[120] Yahya Othman mentions another incident in parliament in July 1967 when Ndobho criticised the employment of expatriate personal secretaries in government. p. 177.

[121] TANU merged with the Zanzibari Afro-Shiraz party in 1977 to form Chama Cha Mapinduzi (Party of Revolution). TANU and its successor CCM have ruled Tanzania since independence.

Zanzibar was different because of the revolution[122] and the whole setup. It may have affected things at the NEC level; it didn't affect them at the village level or the district level. People gradually lost the enthusiasm. It went away because the simple demand for independence was gone, the immediate enthusiasm of building [the country dissipated]. Many people built schools, but then we didn't have teachers. Spontaneity is spontaneity. It doesn't fit very well when you didn't have teachers to put in there, but we didn't have them. We had disappointments like that.

AT: Didn't disappointment lead to people questioning the one-party system?

JW: It wasn't organised. The structure wasn't such that you organised into groups. But they would raise it, you see. But the fact is the teachers are not there,

---

[122] The Zanzibar Revolution took place January 12, 1964, in which 600–800 African militants overthrew the Sultan of Zanzibar and his mostly Arab government. They were frustrated by the underrepresentation of Africans in the parliament even though the Afro-Shiraz Party and Umma Party had won 54% of the vote. The revolt led to many deaths. ASP leader Abeid Karume became the country's new president.

so the district or village chairman would go to his district chairman and would say,

"I have put in for some more teachers. Here is the letter I have written that I have this school; I need some teachers."

But his reply was, "We haven't got any teachers," or

"We will get one at the year's end when they come out of training."

But you don't need one; you need 10 or 3 or 4. And then you won't get them.

AT: You questioned the shift toward the one-party state?[123]

JW: That is my British background.

AT: But then it seems that you changed your mind just as things were getting worse.

JW: I changed my mind reasonably quickly because I saw the system working, and I saw that, for example, Mwalimu, as well as other people were always, I wouldn't say nervous — because that is the wrong word — but they were more worried about what the National Executive [Committee] was going

---

[123] Tanzania was initially a multiparty state at independence. It became a one-party system in 1965 dominated by TANU until 1992, when the constitution reinstated a multiparty system.

to say and how they were going to receive a new proposal than they were about parliament. Members of parliament raised issues, but it was the National Executive [Committee] and the Central Committee that would be challenged. There were people in there that had grown up with Mwalimu in the movement, particularly the older ones. You get up against this age thing. The younger ones [TANU members] couldn't have been so active in the pre-independence struggle as the older ones, and so you had this fact that they didn't have long experience before. They had not worked with the movement before. But also, younger people do not challenge elders.

You had people like Rajabu Diwani,[124] old men, illiterate until the end. He might have just learned to read and write. He would challenge Mwalimu on anything, a very valuable man. Basic fundamental challenges, Mwalimu held him in the highest respect. He knew that he had got to convince him. He would listen, he could be convinced, but he was not dogmatic. He [Diwani] would challenge him [Nyerere]. There were others like him, but he is the

---

[124] Rajabu Diwani was a member of the TANU Central Committee.

one I knew best because he was in Dar es Salaam and I saw him. He was very nice, but he was rough, no-nonsense about him.

In the village, [one found the] same thing. [There] would be a clan leader, a chairman, or some of the chairmen, particularly in the pre-Arusha declaration period, who were beginning to get the extra bit on the farm and building themselves up. Well, just like anybody would do at that level. It was at the higher level they could borrow money from the banks, like Bibi Titi.[125] I never believed that Bibi Titi was fundamentally evil or mistaken or that she had been

---

[125] Bibi Titi Mohammed (1926–2000) had been a close friend of Nyerere and a founding member of TANU. She played a major role in the fight for independence and was known for her rousing speeches. She mobilised large numbers of women to support TANU and to enlist others to join the party. After independence she became the first leader of the TANU's women's union, Umoja wa Wanawake wa Tanzania (UWT), and served as a member of the Central Committee. In 1969 she was charged, alongside Labour Minister Michael Kamaliza and four army officers, with plotting to overthrow the government. She was sentence to life in prison in 1970, but her sentence was commuted in 1972. Her reputation was eventually restored and CCM recognised her as a heroine of the struggle for independence. A street was named after her in Dar es Salaam.

fighting in the nationalist movement to get herself rich. No, I never believed that. No. I just think she was a simple woman.

Somebody comes to her and says, we would like you to become the director of our company, [and she thought] "Well, that sounds great, I can help the workers." So she was asked to be director of some company. I don't know if they were selling helicopters or new machines. There was much talk about a machine that could fly over land and float on top of the water [hovercraft], and so the lack of bridges didn't matter. Then they made her director of this company, and she was talking about "my company" and urging the government to buy whatever these machines were from "my company." I don't believe for a minute [she thought she was doing something wrong]. That woman was being used and exploited like nobody's business. She was innocent in the strongest sense of the word. She did not realise what was happening. She did not realise how she was being exploited. She really did feel that this was [her chance]. She felt that now we are independent, we have Africans in charge, and I am one of them. I don't know if she read any of the papers. She learned English. I helped teach her English when she was standing for election in

1960 when she knew very little indeed. She got better, but I didn't go on with her. She could do it, but it was halting. You can't give her a technical paper or a board agenda, talking about something financial. What is she going to know? It's cruel, but they did it. The banks would come and say, why don't you buy a house, rent it? She would see nothing wrong with it. Then, of course, she was very upset when the Arusha Declaration came along.

AT: But she was not the only one.

JW: No, no, no, there were many other leaders. If we had been as democratic as all that, we would never have got the Arusha Declaration, not because of the people's lack of support but because of the leadership. We had to fight that every inch of the way.

AT: Was there room for debate? I talked to some people on the Central Committee at the time, and they felt there wasn't much room for opposition to the Arusha Declaration.

JW: I probably talked to him [Nyerere] about that and raised questions. What questions I raised, I can't remember, but undoubtedly, we would have talked about that at some point. Sometimes he may have just listened. He listened to everybody. He was a great listener. That is one of the most important things about Mwalimu. I would probe him and probe him more. If he didn't want to [engage], he would just sit and listen. He would sit a while and introduce another subject, or someone would come in, or he would say,

"I must go do some work now. You got your answer."

[This meant] he wasn't going to answer. Either he would agree or disagree.

The Aftermath of the Tanzania-Uganda War

JW: Mwalimu had organised a meeting of all Ugandan groups in Moshi [in March 1979],[126] which had

---

[126] The Moshi meeting was held at the end of the war between Uganda and Tanzania from October 1978 until June 1979. The war led to the overthrow of Ugandan President Idi Amin, who had overthrown President Milton Obote in 1971. Nyerere supported Obote's attempt to launch a rebellion in Uganda in 1972, leading to a border clash and eventual agreement with Amin to withdraw forces from the border. Relations between Tanzania and Uganda remained tense after that. Amin later claimed that a piece of land in Kagera, Tanzania, belonged to Uganda and in October 1978 Ugandan forces started making incursions and eventually invaded Tanzania. On November 2,

decided that Yusuf Lule was the man that would take over [Uganda]. And Obote did not attend.[127] Obote was very angry that Mwalimu backed [the meeting]. After relations between them were very bad, even when he got back into power [in 1980]. Nyerere supported Obote as leader until Amin was overthrown and until Ugandans decided Lule should be president. He did support him until that point because he was the overthrown president. By that time [of the Moshi conference], he didn't agree with Mwalimu at all. Mwalimu urged him to form a government that would include every group in a coalition. Obote rejected it.

Transition of Power to Mwinyi

AT: Did Nyerere regret later on that he had pushed for Mwinyi?

....

Tanzania declared war on Uganda, backed the forces of Obote and Yoweri Museveni, and retook the territory Amin had claimed in Tanzania. They occupied parts of Uganda and ousted Amin in April 1979.

[127] Nyerere persuaded Obote to stay away to avoid the impression that Tanzania was trying to install an Obote government. Obote's party, the Uganda People's Congress, attended the Moshi conference, instead.

JW: He didn't, in fact. He did not. He didn't want Mwinyi to be his successor. He wanted Salim.[128] Mwinyi wasn't a dictator in a sense. Nyerere didn't push for Salim, but it was almost certainly known [that he wanted Salim], and Mwinyi said he didn't want it. He wanted to stay in Zanzibar.

AT: But Salim didn't go through because …

JW: Because of Zanzibar's politics and the fact that he was of Arab descent.[129] That was all private.

AT: That was all between the Zanzibaris. I don't think the mainlanders would have cared so much.

JW: No, I think they would have quite liked it, but the Zanzibaris were quite hot on that. Rashidi

---

[128] Salim Salim had served in numerous ambassadorial positions in Egypt, India, China, Cuba and other countries from 1961 to 1980. He served as representative of Tanzania to the UN (1970–1980), Secretary-General of the OAU (1989–2001), and African Union Special Envoy on the Darfur Conflict (2004–2008). Because he had spent so much time outside of Tanzania, he had limited visibility within the country, although he was certainly well known.

[129] Salim Salim was born in Zanzibar to a father who was an Arab from Oman and a mother who was born in Tanzania and of mixed race (Arab father and Afro-Arab mother).

[Kawawa][130] was the third candidate. There were
three candidates. Rashidi pulled out at the end for
health [reasons]. It is true his health was bad by that
time. He wouldn't have been a good president. He
was very loyal. I had tremendous respect for him.
I liked him. But I mean, he had his limitations too.
He was a good number two. He backed up Mwalimu
in everything. He came from a traditional family.
Perhaps where the boss says do this, and you do
it. He didn't understand necessarily about the way
you do things, so he would go about like a bull in
a china shop when it came to implementing policy.
Not many leaders could have been prime minister.
When he [Nyerere] took over as President in 1962,
Rashidi became Prime Minister. Then when we got

[130] Rashidi Kawawa (1926–2009) helped found the Tanganyika
Federation of Labour (TFL) and was elected as its first general
secretary in 1955. He joined TANU and became a Central
Committee member in 1957 and vice president of TANU in
1960. He was appointed to the Legislative Council in 1957 and
remained a representative until 1960. He served as prime minister
briefly from January to December 1962. He was appointed first
vice president in 1962 and second vice president in 1964 up
until 1972, when he became prime minister again. He remained
as prime minister until 1977. He later held the post of defense
minister from 1977 to 1980. He held the post of secretary general
of CCM from 1982 to 1990.

the union [between Tanganyika and Zanzibar in 1964], he became second vice president instead of first vice president.[131]

The man he wanted [to succeed him as president] was Salim Salim, not Mwinyi. Mwinyi knew this, Salim knew this, but the Central Committee decided on Mwinyi. That has been known for a long time, semi-publicly. One of the things which made him want Salim was because he thought Mwinyi was holding Zanzibar in the union and that he was doing a good job in Zanzibar. He wasn't sure what would happen in Zanzibar when he [Nyerere] left. That was one of his reasons for wanting Salim, probably the largest. He [Nyerere] told Mwinyi, and Mwinyi himself took that line [of supporting Salim].

I remember the Central Committee was meeting in the office just opposite mine, and we all were anxious to know what was happening in there. A colleague of mine came along and said,

"Look, I know who has not got it."

I said, "Who's that and why?"

He said, "Mwinyi looked so miserable, he must have lost. He must have not got the candidacy."

---

[131] The United Republic of Tanganyika merged with Zanzibar on 22 April 1964.

I said, "I think it means he has got it because he doesn't want it."

And it was true, he had got it, and he didn't want it. I personally thought he'd be good, and I remember saying that I thought he was more of a socialist than Salim was. Mwinyi had occasionally used the word socialism and Arusha Declaration. Salim never did.

I think he was a very simple man, a very nice man, and meant extremely well, but I think he could be in a sense inveigled into things. He was very simple. People gave him a present, no strings attached, nothing, and he would accept this, thinking it was just their goodness and generosity and so on. Only afterwards, he would be almost blackmailed. There is no doubt by the end that he was corrupted.

Privatisation and Economic Liberalisation under Mwinyi (1985–1995)

JW: When Mwinyi[132] took over, Mwalimu was very careful not to intervene. For a long time, he wouldn't

---

[132] Ali Hassan Mwinyi (1925–) served as second president of Tanzania 1985–1995 and CCM chairman from 1990 to 1996. Prior to this, he had served as interior minister and vice

even talk about anything domestic at all, but he backed up Mwinyi in the National Executive and Central Committee on the IMF decision, although he tried to urge Mwinyi to use his [Nyerere's] own unpopularity with the IMF.

[He told him,] "This is an opportunity for you to exploit my unpopularity."

Remember that man [Nyerere] was still the chairman of the party. But, in fact, he [Nyerere] did back him [Mwinyi] in that sort of thing.

AT: Why did he back him in going to the International Monetary Fund (IMF)?

JW: Because there was no choice. I mean, you know, we really were in a lot of economic trouble.

AT: He resisted earlier on …

JW: No, he resisted right at the end. He was [then] still fighting. We had constant battles with the IMF. Mwalimu was upset with what they objected to, which has now become common policy. The fact of this litany which they brought from Washington is a litany of devaluation, end of price controls, privatisation,

....

president. During his tenure he introduced policies of economic liberalisation and multipartyism, reversing many of the central policies of Nyerere.

end of all subsidies — all the anti-people policies — which is part of their litany implicitly.

AT: Did Nyerere object to the effects of those policies, or was it also because of the control or loss of sovereignty coming from the outside?

JW: Well, by this time, he had accepted the fact that we needed IMF credit because it was credit we were talking about. We are members [of the IMF]. We were entitled to it. So yes, he objected to that [loss of sovereignty], but no, it was really what the litany was and what its effect would be [on Tanzanians]. He would challenge them on this. I mean tremendous arguments.

You know they would be negotiating with the Ministry of Finance and/or the Ministry of Planning. Sometimes they [the negotiations] were separate; sometimes, they were together. He always insisted he wanted to do it himself and, of course, the minister concerned would be there. He would challenge these people, and they couldn't beat his challenge. They couldn't answer his questions:

"What is this going to do to people? You talk about ending subsidies on fertiliser and those agricultural things. The Europeans have protection of their things; they subsidise, the Americans subsidise. But we mustn't subsidise. Why? Our people are poorer than they are, than their farmers are. You are making their life impossible."

It was on that sort of level.

On privatisation, of course, it was for two reasons. One, the principles of public ownership, but also the fact that we don't have any people with that sort of capital. If you privatise, you are selling all our assets to somewhere else. It wouldn't have been to South Africa at that point. Americans, British, anyone who wasn't Tanzanian. We had a few local small factories. There was one pharmaceutical firm. They had a chemist on the corner by the Askari monument. I can't remember. I'm so bad with names. But anyway, that little pharmacy. I think in the end, I am not sure if it was ever taken over. It was the only one we ever had. Really, they didn't go for the private shops.

AT: With privatisation and economic liberalisation, was there much choice at the point that these policies were adopted?

JW: On the privatisation, they could have got a much better agreement than they did simply by threatening them with Mwalimu, and he kept urging them to do that. Nyerere urged Mwinyi privately but never commented publicly. He did not talk about privatisation. But he would mention it in his remarks, in his speeches. He would say,

"If you want to privatise, then go ahead, but you can't do this with self-reliance. Without self-reliance, you lose everything."

The fact that he didn't like it was known, but he did not campaign on the issue at all.

The Shift Towards Multipartyism (1991)

JW: Mwalimu was the one who started the move toward multipartyism. There was a lot of talk at the university, and some people would form groups [that] they were calling parties. I mean, this was a handful of people. Then he urged the president [to consider moving toward multipartyism]. First, he talked about it when nobody was talking about it, no [CCM] leader, no critical leader. Mwalimu, despite all the things that have been said about him, [he] didn't like things to go underground. He much preferred to bring them out. He could argue anyone into conceding, and very few people had the courage to argue with him. He really admired and liked those who did. One of the reasons he had great respect for [Edwin] Mtei was that Mtei had argued with him.[133] He [Nyerere] didn't come out supporting the multiparty thing at that stage. Mtei had resigned, and I think Mwalimu encouraged him to resign because it was becoming very difficult. You had a finance minister who wanted devaluation and a president who was saying no. Certainly, Mwalimu always respected Mtei. Nobody attacked Mtei or his loyalty or anything else in Mwalimu's presence without being stopped.

AT: Why did Nyerere start to open up for multipartyism, especially because it did not seem that there were strong pressures from Tanzanians to do so?

---

[133] Edwin Mtei was the first Governor of the Bank of Tanzania and the architect of Central Banking in Tanzania, Secretary General of the East African Community, and Finance Minister (1977–79) in Nyerere's government. He resigned from his ministerial portfolio because of differences with Nyerere over the IMF. He eventually went to work for the International Monetary Fund (IMF) and founded the opposition party, CHADEMA (Chama cha Demokrasia na Maendeleo) in 1992.

JW: To the contrary. Before the Nyalali report,[134] there were people raising the question, and the question was being raised by some people at the university.

AT: But there were no mass protests or civil society pressures?

JW: Mwinyi appointed the presidential commission [Nyalali Commission], and after that, it was debated. The Nyalali report came up with about 20 per cent of the people who thought it would be a good idea [to go multiparty]. Mwalimu's reaction to that was, if it is 20 per cent, you've either got to [adopt multipartyism] or smash them, but that would involve a whole different atmosphere, and any development of democracy would have been in limbo. Or if people don't want it, let these people who want to start democracy find out. Then he encouraged this debate. After that, it was debated. Mwalimu stopped being chairman of the party [in 1990]. I think he did five years [as party

---

[134] President Mwinyi had appointed a presidential commission, the Nyalali Commission, to collect public opinions on whether Tanzania should adopt a multiparty system. The commission was headed by then Chief Justice Francis Nyalali, who served as Chief Justice of Tanzania from 1977 to 2000. Based on its 1991 recommendations, the Tanzanian Constitution was amended to institute a multiparty system in Tanzania.

chairman] after Mwinyi took over [as president in 1985]. He was originally going to do only two and a half years. He certainly wasn't surprised by the result. I don't think anyone else was surprised. Still, and even now, I believe the CCM candidate will be elected again with a good straightforward vote. They may lose a few more seats.

Mwalimu was also worried by the fact that the party was becoming slack and losing concern for the people and involvement with the people. He was very concerned with that, and indeed, that was the "but" that was coming up all the time. He never believed, and I think the evidence in Africa and Tanzania was [there,] that multipartyism would reduce or stop or hold a check on corruption. In fact, it doesn't; it makes it worse. No doubt about that at all.

One of Mwalimu's ambitions from very early on, which I can remember him saying, was to build up institutions, build up the whole idea of democratic discussion and debate and so on and have a peaceful transfer of power to his successor. He knew, and indeed, if you look at his speeches before the 1980 election and the party meeting before that, he argued the case for [leaders] standing down [and not running again]. He had been saying publicly that he was going to stand down. The pressure was that you could not. This was partly [out of] fear. No one really wants to go into the unknown. It was partly fear, partly [that] you like old clothes and don't want new ones. [You] only want new ones for special occasions, but you don't want to change your entire dress habits. So equally, [the leaders] were reluctant to do this. In 1980 he made a whole speech making a case for change and said,

"I will serve another five years," which, of course, he did.

That was certainly popular.

There were these voices coming up, and they came up faster after that [demanding that he not run again]. Mwalimu provided some of the arguments. He made an interesting speech — you should try and get it. It was right at the end of his speech, which was quite a long one that he said he would stay on for another five years.[135] That was the end. But then, of course, when we came up to 1985, there were the same pressures [that] he must continue because the economy is a mess. He could have got elected. He may have gone down from 92 or 93 per cent to 80

---

[135] Summarised in "Report on Tanzania—November 1980," FCO 31/2877, PRO (UK National Archives).

per cent, but he would have got there. [Instead] he got this peaceful transfer of power. He really felt that a load had come off his shoulders. He backed [up] Mwinyi all the time.

He made many criticisms, especially toward the end. He attacked some individuals on corruption. He spoke up in public when there was this debate about having three governments: Tanzania, Zanzibar and the Union.[136] He came up very strongly against that. He made a bitter attack on [John] Malecela, in particular, but also for corruption in his case. Alleged corruption. No one has ever managed to get him [Malecela] to court. He is still vice chairman of the party. He was not exactly a great lover of the president. I think he doesn't have Rashidi's perceptions of loyalty, either. But anyway, that's another question. Mwalimu came out publicly and campaigned on those two issues, the Union and corruption. But at no point did he ever criticise President Mwinyi, not even indirectly.

---

[136] The proposed three tier government would have had three presidents, one for the United Republic, a President of Tanganyika and a President of Zanzibar. The three governments proposal was not adopted.

Long before the one-party state came up, the republican constitution was very different. The independence constitution was very much [along] the traditional Whitehall pattern. The republican constitution — and he [Nyerere] was still involved because he was leading the party in 1962, while Rashidi was the prime minister. Mwalimu had resigned from being prime minister on January 22, 1962, [to restructure TANU] before he came back as president [in December 1962] — I know that if you look at the republican constitution, you get your executive president. He doesn't have a cabinet; the prime minister is not there; no mention of the prime minister. We have a president and vice president, of course, this is before the union anyway, and the executive president has enormous powers, I mean almost unlimited powers, except over the judiciary. He has to meet his cabinet and consult with them. They can all say no, but if he says yes, then that is yes [that is what is decided]. This is very different from the British setup, and [this] was a matter of great controversy. [Some said] we were going undemocratic, dictatorship was being established and so on. Well, the constitution would have allowed for a dictatorship, but it didn't become one. I didn't attend cabinet meetings. Mwalimu didn't tell me. Sometimes he would mention [something] in passing, but basically, he didn't tell me what went on in cabinet. I didn't see cabinet papers, except if he gave me one for a particular purpose. He lent me his but then I had to give it back to him. But that was rare. I know that he would, really through the force of his argument and personality, he would get them to acquiesce [if nothing more].

The Arusha Declaration was different.[137] The Arusha Declaration, Mwalimu pushed it through. It was not democratic at all. Bibi Titi was right that it was not democratic. But it never would have happened if it [would have] been democratic. Because people loved it, but the leadership didn't. They didn't for the

---

[137] The 1967 Arusha Declaration was the central document in establishing the egalitarian, self-reliant and socialist orientation that Tanzania had adopted. It resulted in the nationalisation of major financial, commercial and manufacturing institutions. Its Leadership Code was aimed at preventing Party leaders from becoming part of a privileged group that exploited people through hiring labour or renting property. When the Leadership Code was first implemented it was aimed primarily at senior Party and Government leaders and high and middle-ranking civil servants, but gradually it came to apply to all leaders and Party members receiving a salary of over 1,060.70 Tsh.

very reason he had it adopted. Too many of them were beginning to make money, to take off. I mean, he was a democrat, but a democrat who was quite prepared to go over the heads of leaders to the people. But he would always argue. He used to complain sometimes that the ministers did not do it, even the minister of information didn't do it, so time and again …

AT: Do what?

JW: I mean, explain the policy. The people did not understand, so he had to do it himself. He had to explain it.

AT: One of the impressions I got going back over the *Daily News* issues since the 1960s and looking at all that transpired was the patronising way Nyerere's speeches were presented. The headlines read: "Mwalimu tells peasants to grow millet," and "Mwalimu says women should develop." It was paternalistic. Is that an accurate characterisation, or would you challenge that?

JW: I would challenge that it was paternalistic. But I would say the cabinet would agree. Or everybody would know. Economically, it was the thing to do. In times of famine, he pushed millet, which the agriculturalists did not like. I remember Reg Green,[138] who wasn't an agriculturalist, but who was a very good economic advisor, he did a tremendous job. Do you know Reg Green?

AT: Yes, I have seen him with his cat.

JW: Reg is brilliant. He writes more than anybody else I have come across, and it is good stuff. But he cannot write, because he thinks too fast, so he dictates clearly to an extremely good secretary. You can get a sentence that goes on for half a page with clauses and sub-clauses within sub-clauses of sub-clauses, and you've got to sort it out. It is really difficult. Mwalimu and I used to have a joke; we called it "Greenish."

AT: Wasn't he an advisor to Nyerere?

---

[138] Reginald Green (1935–2021) was a development economist based at the Institute of Development Economics at University of Sussex. He was a prolific writer who produced analytical and policy papers on African economic issues, especially on Tanzania, Mozambique and Namibia and the Southern African Development Community (SADC). For seven years Green was economic adviser to the Ministry of Finance. He was known for being a bit eccentric. He wore a small Muslim cap covering his long hair. He sported colorful neckerchiefs tied with a cowrie shell knot and walked around with his cat on his shoulder.

JW: No, not to Mwalimu directly, but to the ministry of finance mostly. Sometimes in economic ministries. Green and Roland Brown[139] did a lot of negotiation. They made a tremendous team. Because Roland, of course, is also very brilliant in his own field and very committed, as Reg was too, I think. Green did not always agree with Mwalimu's policies at all. On devaluation, he wanted devaluation long before Nyerere did. He went on arguing for it. Of course, he combatted Edwin Mtei.[140] If Mtei needed combating, I don't know. Amir also wanted devaluation long before we had it. He was suggesting,

---

[139] Roland Brown (1924–2016) was an English barrister who served as Tanganyika's first attorney general from 1961-1965. He was succeeded as AG by Mark Bomani. He had met Nyerere in Britain when Nyerere was studying there in the 1950s, and later served as a constitutional adviser prior to independence. Nyerere asked him to prepare the 1964 agreement that would govern the union of Zanzibar and the Mainland after Independence. After 1965, he stayed on in Tanzania as Nyerere's adviser on international and commercial legal affairs. He designed the legal framework for the nationalisation of private commercial banks following the 1967 Arusha Declaration.

[140] After leaving government service in Tanzania, Mtei became the chief negotiator for the IMF with Tanzania.

"Let's devalue some before we go to the IMF and World Bank."

And Mwalimu would say, "All they will do is pocket it and make the same sorts of demands anyway."

Amir just went on arguing privately and accepted it. Amir also had the idea that:

"He is the president. My job is to advise him. If I don't like it, and I am not prepared to accept it, I can leave."

He often didn't like it, but he wasn't going to quit. Mwalimu had tremendous respect for him; he liked him. He once said of Amir,

"The trouble with Amir is, he is like Jesus. He takes the troubles of the whole world, of the whole of Tanzania, on his shoulder. He feels everyone's pain and bears it."

Mwalimu had a tremendous feeling for Amir.

So Mwalimu came out publicly and campaigned on those two issues, the union and corruption. But at no point did he *ever* criticise the president [Mwinyi], not even indirectly. When he took on the whole leadership and the judiciary and so on for corrupting people, [he did so privately]. Privately, he would talk about how people can't get justice because of the corruption of the judiciary, but he did not go into those details. He just attacked the principle of corruption and the fact that it was now widespread. Because obviously, we had problems of corruption while he was president. He tried a few times to get a few court cases, but as always, with corruption, it is very difficult to get a court case. There was one judge he tried to get rid of, and the chief justice pointed out to him that he had no power to get rid of him. Mwalimu said, "but he is corrupt; you deal with him."

AT: Nyalali, when he retired, made a big speech on corruption and the judiciary in his outgoing speech.

JW: Well, he didn't help Mwalimu when Mwalimu was trying to get rid of corruption at an earlier stage. Maybe he didn't think it was widespread. I don't know. I didn't know him well. I knew him obviously, but I didn't know him well. He was always very loyal.

At the beginning, Mwinyi used to consult him [Nyerere] a lot.[141] Mwalimu would ask questions and send his questions back to him, with his comments inherent in the questions. Well, I was never there, obviously. [Andrew] Daraja — he was the one who took over for me [as Mwinyi's personal assistant and

---

[141] Nyerere was party chairman during Mwinyi's first term 1985-1990.

speech writer] — he saw Mwinyi a lot inevitably. I
didn't have much personal contact [with Mwinyi],
but we [Daraja and I] were very concerned that
nothing we did would ever get the two men into
a situation where they would conflict by saying
different things on the same issue. We would consult
on major speeches. We saw the danger, and indeed
it came up again in Mwalimu's speech in 1990, that
if the two leaders quarrel, their staff will be vying for
supremacy and power. It didn't occur. Like I said, he
was very loyal to Mwinyi. He had his differences, but
he didn't go and criticise him at all. Either publicly
or privately. But some of the things he said privately,
he knew, and I knew, were really forbidden. Mwinyi
would not be [have been] pleased at all.

Then, of course, when Mwinyi passed over [the
presidency to Benjamin Mkapa], there was some talk
at one point about changing the constitution so that
Mwinyi could benefit, and he stopped it; he [Nyerere]
just jumped on that. But [he] did not do it publicly.
[Nyerere] talked [with him] about the principles of
not changing the constitution, but only privately and
in the party did he talk against the policy of three
terms. Mwinyi himself, if you notice, never himself
came out and said, "No." He didn't particularly say

"yes," but he didn't say "no." When the kite flying was going on, he didn't stop it as he could have done.

Mwalimu fought against corruption. The fact that you could not display wealth was, of course, a help. You had to pretend you didn't have wealth if you were corrupt, at least to any significant extent. Of course, your wife could have gold rings and bracelets and so on, but it was not enough to have a major inquiry in any case. He once tried to purge the police, but he later had to retire the person who had been actually doing the purging because he got rid of all the honest ones. It's difficult who judges the judges.

AT: It is a difficult situation when people are not being paid a living wage. It makes liars out of everyone, even people who do not want to, who wouldn't otherwise lie.

JW: I always understood, but I didn't approve. But you know, [there was] your messenger who lost the file until you gave some *chai* [a bribe]. No one ever asked me for it. I was working for Mwalimu, so you didn't do it. It was the ministers, the big ones, that I was really upset about. When you get the sort of wedding — this was long after Mwalimu's time and which I was certainly not prepared for in Mwalimu's time

— when Kahama's[142] son or daughter[143] married the
son or daughter of John Rupia.[144] That wedding was
disgusting, really disgusting. Mwalimu, fortunately,
ensconced himself in Butiama[145] at the time and
didn't come. Everybody was invited, all the people
at the senior level were invited. The only people at
the senior level who were not invited were Charles
Sanga[146] and me. It was not because we didn't know

---

[142] George Kahama was nominated in 1957 to the Tanganyika
Legislative Council (LEGCO), representing West Lake Province.
After 1958, he was an elected member of parliament. He was
General Manager and CEO of the National Development
Corporation, the largest holding company in Tanzania from
1966–1973. He held numerous ministerial posts, including
Minister for Home Affairs, Minister of Commerce and Industry,
Communications, Transport and Works and Minister for
Cooperatives and Marketing. He served as Minister of State in
the President's Office and as Director-General of the Capital
Development Authority and planned the building of the new
capital in Dodoma. He also held diplomatic appointments in
Germany, China and Zimbabwe.

[143] Anna Kahama Rupia.

[144] John Rupia was a businessman. He became the first TANU
Vice President and treasurer.

[145] Butiama is the natal home of Nyerere in northern Tanzania.

[146] Charles Sanga held numerous diplomatic posts, including
ambassador to China and representative to the Tanzania
Permanent Mission to the United Nations in New York. In 1992

both of them [Kahama and Rupia]. Most of the ministers went if not all. I don't know; I was not there. I mean, this was a huge thing. They must have spent millions. Parties before, separately, parties together, the wedding itself; 5,000 people invited. Sit down dinner, liquor. You can't do that on the salary of the head of a civil service or the head of NDC.[147] Anyway, then, of course, Ben [President Benjamin Mkapa] came in.[148] Ben managed to stay honest, although he was a minister, also. Several times I said to him,

....

he took the post of Personal Assistant to Nyerere for seven years. He also worked as a part-time lecturer at the Centre for Foreign Relations. He served as, Diplomatic Advisor to President Jakaya Kikwete in 2006. He was appointed Deputy Permanent Secretary in the Ministry of Foreign Affairs and International Cooperation until 2008 when he retired.

[147] National Development Corporation

[148] Benjamin Mkapa (1938–2020) was the third president of Tanzania (1995–2005). He was also chairman of the CCM. He started out as an administrative officer in Dodoma and Minister for Science, Technology and Higher Education. He served as managing editor of the government-controlled *Nationalist* and party-run *Uhuru* newspapers from 1966 to 1972, when he took over the government paper, *Daily News* and *Sunday News*. In 1974, President Nyerere appointed him as his press secretary and he became the founding director of the Tanzanian press agency, *Shihata* (Shirika la Habari Tanzania). He headed the Tanzanian

"Ben, you ought to resign. This government is going and doing these things? Corruption, covered with the mud of other people."

He never was really firm. Anyway, he's now [been] struggling against it; he has retired a number of people in the public's interest. He has had one or two court cases, but not yet against anyone really serious. He was hoping that the Warioba report[149] would help.

AT: What happened with that [the Warioba report]?

JW: Lots of things happened, but not in the case of taking people out because there was no evidence there. I mean, I don't know; I have not read it.

AT: I have read it. There are no names. They say people in this ministry or that, but again there are no dates, no names.

JW: You can't take people to court on that.

AT: The problem with that report was that corruption was everywhere; it was everything. There was nothing specific.

....

mission to Canada in 1982 and to the United States in 1983–84. Mkapa served the Minister of Foreign Affairs from 1977 to 1980 and again from 1984 to 1990.
[149] The Presidential Commission on Corruption (Warioba Commission).

JW: Mwalimu was looking forward to that in the hopes that it would give him that. There are an awful lot of people at the senior level who have been retired in the public's interest. But you can't do anything about elected leaders, elected MPs, unless you have some evidence which can stand [up] in a courtroom.

NYERERE'S LEADERSHIP ETHOS

Clientelism in President's Inner Circle?

JW: You were talking yesterday about why I wasn't surprised that one party became particularly corrupt, not in money terms, but in power terms to a large extent. I said I thought this was just adrift, partly because I think Tanzanians are too good-natured; they don't stick up for themselves. That is not universally true, of course, but they have a tendency of going along with things: "The TANU secretary said this," "The TANU chairman said that." It is not the culture, I suppose, of standing up and having a fight. I don't mean a physical fight. Mostly, they gave way until it became impossible and then they would come and try to see Mwalimu or somebody else. That is how all sorts of things got discovered.

Because the door was kept open as wide as possible, some people would go and see Mwalimu's sister. He had three sisters [at the beginning]. One died not long after independence. But then the other two were left; Nyangeta was his senior who was very intelligent, but I think she was just about literate, certainly did not read. She had been divorced. Her child had died, but she really adopted just about all the children there were. She first looked after other people's children and later actually adopted children. They were a family of six. She looked after these kids right until she was in her 70s. She was concerned about the ones she had adopted later. One or two of them stayed to help her. She was quite a woman. But she would go to Mwalimu and say, "So and so tells me; I am going to bring him to see you." She was a good conduit of problems. And people from all over Tanzania would find themselves eventually getting to Butiama or Dar es Salaam [to see Nyerere].

AT: Did Nyerere use his position to do favours for friends?

JW: When he could, he helped, particularly people who had been very active. He didn't put people in jobs who were not qualified, but he would sometimes say to one member of staff, "See if you can find a job" or "Get national housing to give her a flat." That was rare, and we would then try. We didn't always succeed. People in National Housing knew that "This is a request." I remember one time when I called up National Housing on his behalf to request housing for a relative; they turned me down flat.

Ethnicity in the Military

AT: Colonel Swai, who had written about the military, said many of the top positions in the military were held by people from Nyerere's part of the country. Is that true?

JW: That is traditional. The British army practically consisted of Wakuria, in particular, and indeed after the mutiny, an endeavour was made to get quotas from each region so as to avoid that [a concentration of one ethnic group], or to counter that.[150] The Kuria were bright people, I mean, I'm not generalising, but basically, those that really wanted to get into the army would go down to Mbeya. You didn't ask what tribe they were. It was contrary to policy to ask what tribe they were, so if somebody signed up in Mbeya, it would

---

[150] Nyerere was from the Wazanaki tribe in Butiama. The Wazanaki are related to the Wakuria.

turn out to be a Kuria who went down there for that purpose. It was a tradition among those people. I think there was another tribe for whom it was traditional; Hehe, I think. It was just part of the culture.

Ethnicity in Tanzania

AT: What do you think are some of the reasons Tanzania has held together?

JW: One is policy, one is the language.

AT: That is an obvious one.

JW: I think there's an advantage in the fact that we had 123 tribes; that is the official figure. Some are similar to ones nearby, but they were different. They had their own languages. That was important; it helped people because no one could dominate. In Kenya, you had the Kikuyu, who were the largest tribe around the capital who absorbed the capitalist sort of "I want to get rich, I can get rich" ethos. The Zaramo[151] were not particularly well-educated. I don't know how big they are; we never looked, we didn't take those

---

[151] The Zaramo were historically the largest single group living around the capital of Dar es Salaam.

kinds of statistics when I was there. But we did know they were Muslim by and large, and they didn't get much in the way of mission education. There were some government schools, of course. Probably more than other places. But you weren't overwhelmed with educated people. They had traditional education, but not modern education. The best-educated people were obviously the Chagga, possibly the Wahaya to a lesser extent, both of whom had been heavily missionised. But they were both a long way from Dar es Salaam. I don't know how big the Wahaya population was.

AT: But the Chagga were a very small group, 3 per cent of the population?

JW: Exactly. So, the best-educated were scattered. From the beginning, TANU emphasised that tribe and religion were irrelevant in the demand for independence. It was the policy when they started sending area secretaries or district secretaries, or whatever they were called in those days [of the party], to an area or region. [They did] not send somebody from the village or the area, or the district, [to their home area]. They came with this popular message of independence, and they obviously got local groups coming out before them to develop this. So again, you see, it went [cut] across tribe. That was policy. Later it was loosened, but that went on for a long time. Tribe was never asked. People knew it [not to ask]. In the ministries, you never had both the minister and the principal secretary (PS) from the same tribe, by policy. There was one time that Mwalimu made a change one week of the principal secretary and the next week of the Minister, and he wasn't thinking particularly about this issue, but when he woke up and realised a day or two after that he had two people from the same tribe leading one ministry, the principal secretary was immediately removed. But it was never an issue.

AT: What about religion? Was that the same thing, where they took care that there would not be a buildup of too many Christians or Muslims?

JW: No, it was the same thing. In the political appointments, that would be watched very carefully. It was watched carefully in the cabinet and other political appointments. For a long time, if there was a Muslim qualified to do a more senior civil servant's job and there also were several Christians, the Muslim would probably get the job because there weren't enough of them. There weren't so many educated Muslims. But it was never made an issue. AMNUT[152] tried to make it an issue. Mwalimu simply

---

152 Muslim National Union of Tanganyika (AMNUT)

went on the radio and explained why AMNUT was wrong, that they were dividing the country and so on. I think they took some other steps against AMNUT, but eventually, they banned it. But long before that, there was preparation of people for this, saying,

"This is not anti-Muslim [suppression of the group], it is anti a group which is trying to break down the unity [of the country]."

That was true from the beginning. Mwalimu once said,

"You don't think in tribal terms in making appointments, but you don't ignore them in making appointments, and in the end, you might check." As I said in this one case, he forgot to check it.

AT: What model was he working from?

JW: I don't know of that. Because he was aware. He was not stupid; the British and the French, and the Portuguese had all exploited tribal differences. They brought them [tribal differences] into the modern world instead of letting them sort of die down a bit. They used them certainly. Mwalimu would often say that for the Zanaki,[153] the Maasai were [seen as] the enemy because they came and raided their cattle. He said not in his generation, but his father

---

[153] Nyerere's tribe

and other elders talked about the Maasai; there was a suspicion of the Maasai. [This] didn't worry Mwalimu because he knew the history [which] was there before colonialism, and colonialism perhaps dampened it down in that sense. Sometimes it was exploited by local people in local elections; it cropped up in local disputes, and sometimes again, you had problems with borders.

Under Mwinyi, I was quite shocked when I went back after being away for a couple of years. I left in 1994, Mwinyi came in in 1985. I was shocked when I returned that people were talking about tribes again. They never used to do that. It was almost a taboo subject. They would joke with one another about it, but it was only jokes. You never used to hear under Mwalimu the sort of "Oh, these Wachagga are doing this, and all these others are doing that." But you were hearing it now. I mean, the anti-Asian thing resumed, of course, which had been undercut by the public ownership. It was the way you dealt with this problem of anti-Asian feeling because they were dominating economic life.

Of course, many Tanzanians would know the tribe by the name or the accent of Swahili or so on, but nobody ever talked about it. I don't remember it coming up at all. I honestly don't know who [from what tribe] [Habibu] Halahala was, Mwalimu's press secretary. I have no idea except that he was a Muslim. That I know because he went off to the mosque to pray on a Friday. Paul Sozigwa was a Mzaramo, wasn't he? That you know because he was from the area.

AT: African leaders have often recruited people closest to them to sensitive positions. Did Nyerere do that?

JW: No. [This happened in] the private offices, I suppose. He tended to do this, you know because his was very much a private office. You were out of the mainstream civil service. [These] were people he had come across and knew at some point in his life, but really it is because he wanted a private staff, and it was a personal relationship, not the sort of normal civil service. But they were nearly all, in fact, from the civil service, seconded to him for a while and certainly not all were Kuria, in fact, very few. I think Joseph [Butiku][154] was one. It was a small

---

[154] Joseph Butiku is Executive Director and Trustee of the Nyerere Foundation. He had been one time General Secretary of the CCM in the Mara region and later became the Regional Commissioner. He was President Nyerere's Personal Research Assistant, as well as Chief of Staff and Personal Envoy. He later

tribe anyway, but I think that was the geography. Of course, they had to be educated people because that was the kind of service you wanted. So you had areas where the number, proportion of children who go to school is small. It is small in that East lake region. I am just thinking of the ones we had there. It would have been very much against the policy to ask what tribe somebody was.

AT: Tanzania is very different in that regard.

JW: But in practice, they were slipping into that direction [of tribalism] under Mwinyi.

Evaluating *Ujamaa*[155]

AT: I see you have Susan Geiger's book here.[156] What did you think of it?

-----

become Principal Private Secretary and Chief of Staff under President Ali Hassan Mwinyi.

[155] *Ujamaa* was Tanzania's socialist policy as formulated by Nyerere. It was based on the idea of the nation as family and egalitarianism.

[156] Geiger, Susan. *TANU Women: Gender and Culture in the Making of Tanganyikan Nationalism, 1955–1965* (Heinemann, 1997).

JW: I didn't agree at the end when [Geiger] was summing up. A lot of her stuff I didn't agree with, but I was fascinated by her book. Her attitude again that *Ujamaa* was a failure, I don't accept, and that it was economically disastrous, I still don't accept.

MLS: You had said that you don't accept this when they say *Ujamaa* was a failure, even though it was economically disastrous.

JW: No, I don't accept it.

MLS: Could you just say why not?

JW: First, I think they are looking at *Ujamaa* as a failure, simply because of GDP statistics, whereas *Ujamaa* was much bigger than that. It was about the whole life of ordinary people and who controls what and the well-being of people in the villages, which did not necessarily reflect very much in government statistics on the basis of trade. Of course, there were also restrictions on imports, which was not part of *Ujamaa*, but part of the style of government, which I also agree with. [Nyerere] knew that when he stood down that they would have to have an agreement with the IMF. He had been fighting not for the IMF agreement, but the conditions [under which] they were imposed, which he rejected. And he believed that Mwinyi coming in would make them give him better conditions in order to strengthen him against Nyerere because Nyerere was still chairman of the party. He said to the new president, use me as your bogey man. Say [to the IMF]:

"I can't do that because there will be big trouble from Nyerere if I do that. Therefore, you have got to give me better conditions than this."

Now I don't think that the president [Mwinyi] ever did this, or if he did, he wasn't very good at it. He didn't try and get assistance. Mwinyi didn't do it. But the president backed him up in the party because Mwalimu forced through the acceptance of Mwinyi's agreement even though he wasn't very happy with it. He thought he could have got better conditions. But he never made that public at all. In the party conference, when they had to accept this, he fought it. But publicly, he never criticised the president on this or even on the privatisation issue, which, of course, he didn't like. But he accepted it, and he did say to the people later, not straight away,

"If you want to abandon nationalisation and public ownership, go ahead and do it; it is up to you. You are in charge."

He said this publicly in front of the press, and everybody else who was around, or could have been.

I can't remember if they reported it, but he then said, "What you can't abandon is state independence and the policy of self-reliance." Mwalimu had been pushing that, but he had never been 100 per cent successful. If you look at his farewell speech to the party conference, he said that. We have not had enough self-reliance, and this has been one of our mistakes, but he said, you can't abandon this because this is what your independence is all about. That is one of the things he criticised the president for publicly. Not by name; he never attacked him by name. He attacked the government on that particular aspect. But there is no doubt at all that he didn't like the Zanzibar Declaration[157] when they dropped it. Mwinyi did.

The Arusha Declaration was never put out or abandoned. The policy of *Ujamaa kujitegemea*[158] was still the official policy of the country. One of my

---

[157] The CCM abandoned the 1987 Leadership Code of the Arusha Declaration, in what came to be known as the Zanzibar Declaration of 1991. It challenged the original objectives of the document, particularly the efforts to minimise the gaps between the rich and the poor.

[158] Self-reliance

colleagues who I was friendly with, said that he had spoken to the president [and asked]:

"Did he realise what he had done in Zanzibar?"

The president said, "No, no, we didn't do that."

But, of course, they had done it because they had loosened [the Leadership Code] to the extent that it didn't exist anymore for any practical purposes. But he [Nyerere] didn't publicly criticise Mwinyi. He criticised [what was happening to] self-reliance, he criticised on corruption and then he fought also on the question of three governments, more towards the end when it was Malecela[159] he was fighting, not the president. He accepted the fact that there were going to have to be changes.

MLS: What do you understand by ujamaa when you say *ujamaa* was not a failure? You mean nationalisation?

---

[159] John Malecela was prime minister and first vice president of Tanzania from 1990 to 1994. He served as CCM vice chairman from 1995 to 2007 and was a member of the CCM Central Committee. He was Tanzania's permanent representative to the UN from 1964–1968. He held several diplomatic positions, including being ambassador to Ethiopia, UK, and the Organisation of African Unity. He also held several ministerial posts, including Minister of Foreign Affairs (1972–1973). He was Regional Commissioner of Iringa (1980–1984) and most recently Chancellor of the Open University of Tanzania.

JW: I mean that. But it is not only that. I mean that in the villages, he was concentrating on getting development, schools, clinics, and getting the people to do things for themselves, regardless of what it did to the GDP and so on. It was people's development he was concerned about and the fact of the government being the people's government. I think it was this feeling that the government is on your side. They may make mistakes, they may not do it right and so on, but they are basically on your side, which is important, and it has kept the peace until now.

There were times he admitted, that we had been living on capital. He was saying this even while he was still president at the end, "We are living on capital because the economy is so bad." He didn't think of himself as an economist. He had certain basic principles and certain basic beliefs about the economy. He didn't like if you remember, the socialist Ruvuma Development Association, that sort of thing. He said, even if you could prove to me we would produce more by having bigger estates, by private ownership of agriculture and so on, and plantations, I would not support it. Because the number of actual goods produced would be increased perhaps, but what would be decreased would be the welfare of the people because there would be a gap developing between the amount which is produced and the amount that the peasants themselves can actually eat and drink. And, it was this sort of idea, improving their own quality [of life], producing for themselves, and, in fact, they did not need to sell it all. They could sell it if they wanted to, but they didn't have to. Simply to get maybe some food for themselves or pay taxes.

AT: But what went wrong? They were forced to work in common fields, and this did not work out.

JW: They never did it. That didn't go very far. But he wanted that, and he wanted it done properly. I think one of the great problems Mwalimu had that he didn't recognise, I would say probably to a sufficient extent, is the lack of committed and understanding socialists in the villages and in leadership, particularly at the bottom, but even at the top. One of the things I had forgotten, and I was recently reminded of, was the fact that the leadership really didn't like the Arusha Declaration at all. Many of them fought it and went on fighting it, even the top leadership. Because it did hold them back. So, he went over their heads directly to the people. That was very popular. One of the two things that made it popular was the fact that the Leadership Code was the bit they [the people] liked the most, and leaders hated the most. The other aspect was public ownership. And, on that again, he would have had hardly any of the industrial development which we did have, and which was increasing, not very efficiently, but it was there. We were producing things, mostly because of government investment, because the goods were publicly owned.

I can remember not long after the Arusha Declaration, a year or so after the Arusha Declaration, meeting the then head of the National Development Corporation, the effective executive head, and asking him,

"Is it true that you are not getting foreign investment because of the Arusha Declaration?"

He said we never had any before, the NDC was trying to get it, and we couldn't get it. The only thing we ever succeeded in getting was the drive-in cinema. I don't regard that as being much of foreign investment, although it was a foreign investment. But other than that, we never got anything. What we got after the Arusha Declaration was the General Tires, which was privately owned and was a foreign investment. Phillips was another one. These were all done after the Arusha Declaration.

It wasn't the Arusha Declaration that was keeping them out. The cement factory was there before. In almost the same week after the Arusha Declaration, [Nyerere] opened it and took it over at the same time. That had come in. But it was partly an extension of the one in Kenya. And then they had to push on that too before that could come, but that was before the Arusha Declaration. Really, what stops a great deal of foreign investment, then and now, is the fact that we are a very underdeveloped country, and we don't have the infrastructure that supports a highly productive and efficient industry.

I think it is a big problem, and in a sense, it is a problem of getting Mwalimu's policies on *Ujamaa kujitegemea* actually operating. He could talk directly to people, he was never afraid of them, and he was always happy to respond to their questions. But people with less self-confidence, you have to remember, leaders in Tanzania, the civil service as well as politicians, were people who had very little formal education; by and large, at the time of independence, there were virtually none who had a university education. I remember knowing all the Tanzanians who were in the administrative section class of this civil service; there were so few. It is no longer true, but it was true then. These were the people you were depending upon [to run the country]. They had to cooperate with others with very little experience and very little education, so inevitably, they were all collected at the centre because from the centre, you are guiding policy directions and running the ministries. If you want to Africanise, these are the only people you have that you start with. Given the Arusha Declaration, Mwalimu had to go over the heads of these sort of second, third, if not your fourth layers of leadership to get down to the people. But the people at these various levels were going to have to do the actual implementation, and many of them, I think, genuinely tried.

I think this was one of the problems which Mwalimu completely underestimated. I was never any help to him in this because, in a sense, it was being critical of people I thought were trying hard and doing, in some cases, some things exceptionally well in trying to carry out these policies. It is not surprising that even though many of them tried and did a reasonable job, it was a problem that the people didn't have the background and self-confidence and the mental equipment, not mental ability but mental equipment, to carry these policies out in the way he was thinking of them. He couldn't do it all himself. Not only was he depending upon them to do it, he was also depending on them to report what they were doing. He had all these problems.

Going back to the question, "Why did people respect Mwalimu after all this time?" It was because they knew —in a sense, I am summing up what I am saying—they knew he was on their side; he was working for them, not for himself, not for other leaders. They may have not always agreed; they didn't always agree, particularly when it affected them personally. They didn't necessarily like it. Some of them may have gone into the opposition, not necessarily organised opposition, but I mean they would become opposed to him, but they respected him always.

Then, there was among the intellectuals at the University towards the end of the 1980s, a very small minority that said it would be good when Mwalimu does go. They weren't saying this openly. Also, one senior ambassador said he thought it was right for Mwalimu not to stand again in 1985. The others were saying you must stand again. From the University, we were getting quite a lot of this nonsense that we must join the IMF and we must privatise. Nyerere greatly respected this man with whom he had disagreed.

AT: Who are you referring to?

JW: I don't want to use his name because I don't know if he wants it known that he did it [opposed Nyerere running for office in 1985]. He was an ambassador. But in this case, Mwalimu agreed with him anyway. But he was the only person, apart from myself. I backed him on this [decision not to run again], but that was much less important than the fact that some senior ambassador was taking this line openly. I don't know how open he was to other people, but to Mwalimu, he was very frank, and he argued his case. In Mwalimu's case, he was determined not to stand. He had originally said [that] he had intended to step down in 1980.

People thought he was on their side if there was injustice taking place. Of course, there was much [injustice]. It wasn't because of him. It wasn't what he intended. They knew that. He was constantly travelling in the country, less in the last year because he started going around and saying goodbye, and dealing with the United Nations, and [visiting] people he had never visited. We did a lot of travelling around, not as much as we did with the South Commission.

But in the last year, we visited 17 countries. He was chairman of the Organisation of African Union that last year too, so this meant that he couldn't spend as much time travelling [in Tanzania]. But he still did quite a bit.

He would come into a village and stand on the Land Rover, and he would talk and invite questions, and he would then say,

"Yesterday you took me up to this [place], and there were lots of people working there. I drove by there this morning, and there was nobody working there at all. Why are you trying to pretend? It is dishonest. It is not what you are really doing."

He would challenge the chairman, "Why are you doing this? You took me there. You obviously organised all these people to be there. Why?"

And you know, obviously, the people had known that. They thought he would be taken in, but he wasn't.

His staff, particularly his security staff, also used to sort of go to the bar at the end of his safari for the day. He would usually stay in district headquarters. Not always, and they would come and say,

"You know that place you went to yesterday? Well, it isn't like that according to all the local people. This is what they say is going on."

And then he picked up [information] from all sorts of places. They were very good on that sort of thing. They weren't doing it as security. To my understanding, nobody ever thought that was what they were doing. On the contrary, they were trying to bring to Mwalimu's attention attempts to hoodwink him. I am not saying they [the villagers] were never successful. But they were often not, and people began to realise that. So people felt that Mwalimu was a fair man.

Foreign Diplomats

JW: Whenever I went to see an American or talked to a British High Commissioner, in particular, of course, I would go back and report to Mwalimu. I was telling him what was going on, but incidentally, I was telling him what I was doing and how I knew what I was telling him. Only once I did not repeat some statement by a British High Commissioner because I was so ashamed of it. It was so horrible. It was a remark about Africans. I just couldn't do it. I was so ashamed. They talked to me because I was somehow British and as if I was on their side. I was horrified; I couldn't bear it. That was not true of all of them.

One of them started calling me Joan from the first moment he met me. Publicly and otherwise, he was calling me Joan. Most people called me Joan, most people of my age, but I resented it coming from the British High Commissioner. In the end, I called him in to see me. I said,

"Would you please stop calling me Joan, my name is Miss Wicken."

After that, he used to say "*Miss* [emphasis] Wicken," but when he left, he was quite sorry. I thought he was quite good. He was actually posted to South Africa, and he refused to go, so he was posted to Singapore. It wasn't exactly a promotion. Going to South Africa would have been a big promotion. He said,

"It is time I left Tanzania. I am beginning to think I know Tanzanian politics better than the Tanzanians [and that is not good]."

That was a very rare admission. This other man, who called me Joan, knew how Tanzania should be governed from the day he arrived.

Confidants, Colleagues, and Collaborators

JW: Mwalimu had lots of friends. He saw Amir a lot, but he couldn't relax with Amir. Amir never really relaxed. Well, that is not entirely true. After his second marriage, he learned to play bridge. That was the only way he relaxed. Mwalimu didn't play bridge. Amir was always trying to persuade Mwalimu and me to play bridge so that there would be a foursome. Of course, Mwalimu was not interested in playing bridge, and I was not interested in playing bridge, and that never happened.

AT: What about Derek Bryceson?[160] He was someone in government who was mentioned more than anybody when I was going around in the Coastal region and talking to people, even though he had died several years earlier.

---

[160] Derek Bryceson (1922–1980) was appointed Assistant Minister for Social Services in 1957 by the colonial government but he resigned to support TANU in the elections, winning a seat in the Northern Province. Later he was a member of Tanzania's national assembly, representing Kinondoni District. He held numerous ministerial appointments, including Minister for Mines and Commerce (1959), Health and Labour (1960), Health (1964) and Agriculture (1964). He was appointed Minister for Agriculture and Cooperatives again in 1971 and director of national parks in 1972. He was enormously popular among the electorate. He ran four times for a parliamentary seat and won the largest majority in any constituency in the country in his last election. He married the famous primatologist Jane Goodall in 1975.

JW: He was tremendously popular. He was MP for Manzese. Everybody else was talking about people of Manzese as prostitutes and thieves, and he would go out and sort of visit the bars and join in the conversation. His Swahili was very colloquial when he wanted it to be. He had a tremendous, outgoing personality. He got along very well with people. They knew him. Again they liked him. He certainly was no socialist. But you know he did a good job. But, you know, he was tremendously popular. I think he always got the largest majority [in elections]. You know we have this system of two MPs, two internal candidates. Derek always finished up with a bigger majority than anybody else in the country. He was very much liked. They even asked his son to take over when he died simply because they liked him so much. Mwalimu liked him; everyone liked Derek. But [Mwalimu] did not have the same feeling for him that he had for Amir.

AT: Apart from Jamal, who else was close to Nyerere?

JW: TANU people. Bhoke Munaka[161] was also very friendly right at the beginning, but this was the hangover of nationalism.

---

[161] Bhoke Munaka served as the personal assistant to Nyerere after 1970. He started out as the vice president of the Tanganyika African Association, the precursor to TANU, which he joined

A great friend who pulled back himself because he might have been a junior minister the first time around but didn't last long as a minister, Dossa Aziz, who was a Muslim, not particularly educated.[162] He went into partnership on a farm with John Rupia at one time. He tried to build up a co-op. In practice, he was a very down to earth person; I wouldn't say a peasant because he was more developed and more aware of the world. He had been very active in politics. He was on the Central Committee for a long time, and he used to drop in before Mwalimu became chief minister, prime minister and so on, he would often meet him, and they would go to the Cosy Café.

----

when it was formed in 1954, becoming the party's national treasurer in 1958. He held numerous governmental positions, including Minister of State in the Second Vice President's office, head of the Central Establishment Division in charge of civil service training and organisation and Minister of State for Regional Administration. According to Paul Bjerk, an extensive set of his TANU files at TNA are one of the richest archival collections of the mid-1960s political history.

[162] Dossa Aziz was from a wealthy and cultured family that was originally from Tanga. His father, Aziz Ali Dossa, was the first African to own a car and worked as a building contractor. He built many mosques in Dar es Salaam. Dossa was among the 17 founders of TANU and one of the financiers of the party.

Sometimes I would meet him. That was the place we sat down with him. Dossa used to come.

But then the security people at the gate started saying, "Who are you and what do you want and why?" And Dossa was very proud, so when Mwalimu realised he had not seen him for some time, he sent for him to get him brought in. But Dossa only had political ideas. He was basically a nationalist and went along with socialism without any problem at all. He was not one of the leaders who had been trying to benefit from anything. But because of Dossa's pride and [therefore] his inability to get in, and because he just wouldn't come to Msasani[163] because he was going to meet the security at the gate, he stopped coming.

But when I knew him first, which was in 1957, he took us down to Mbeya in his jeep. It might have been a Land Rover. He carefully looked after you. He was fun. He was working for TANU. If he had an office, he had an office. If he didn't, he didn't worry. He just went on. He wasn't able to give the mental stimulation. He didn't challenge Mwalimu. He made some snide remarks. Well, not snide, because that sounds bad, but sort of pointed remarks, in a good

---

[163] Nyerere's private residence was in Msasani.

joking way. It was a friendly relationship. They saw a lot of each other.

Mwalimu had a lot of friends. Mwalimu relaxed by himself, translating texts into Swahili, writing Swahili verses and reading, thinking, and listening. Lots of people went there in the evening to Msasani, lots of people who on this basis claimed to be great friends. Amir wasn't the only one, but he was in a special place.

NYERERE'S LEGACY

Influence on Tanzania's Politics after 1990

AT: What was Nyerere's influence on Tanzania's politics after he was no longer president?
JW: It depends entirely on the president. If they went and asked him to discuss things, this was always just between people. But I think that probably Mwinyi did depend upon him for backing the party for a long time until he stopped being president. He [Nyerere] was chairman of the party for quite a long time; about five years after he stepped down. But until that point, certainly, Mwinyi needed Mwalimu to back him in the party.

Mwinyi came under pressure from the British, in particular [Prime Minister] Mrs Thatcher, who one time came there on a state visit. There was a lunch that was given for Mwalimu before he stepped down, and they had agreed on no speeches. But Mwinyi did have a prepared speech [quite rightly], but Mwalimu didn't have a prepared speech. This time she made a speech, and she attacked Mwalimu. Mwinyi simply went ahead and read out his prepared speech. It was afterwards that the Tanzanian government, through diplomatic terms, let [it be] known that this [speech by Thatcher] was resented very much. I have no idea whether Mwinyi himself wanted this or how it came up, but they did do it, and, in fact, a visit was made later by a senior British minister, not, of course, the prime minister, who apologised for that.

But I think that it may be [that] Mwinyi had been taunted as being under the control of Mwalimu, and certainly no human being would like that. But they [Mwinyi and Nyerere] always met when Mwalimu came to Dar es Salaam. In the early stages, they [Mwinyi] quite often went to Butiama, which he didn't have to do. What went on between the two is between those two. Mwalimu did not write anything down. I don't know if Mwinyi did; I doubt it. But certainly, I have no idea what went on.

Occasionally Mwalimu would mention, or sometimes I would ask, did you talk to the president about something or other. He might say "yes," or he might say "no," but he certainly wouldn't tell me what he said. Sometimes I would guess because I knew what his feelings were. But he only talked about things having to do with corruption, self-reliance and the union. [It was] very rare for him to bring anything else up, and if he did, he brought it up as a thing he might want to consider. He was not saying you ought to be doing this. Mwalimu was very sensitive on this point. On those three subjects, he might have held a press conference after he was no longer president. Never on anything else. He would never have done it on anything else. The union he was concerned with.

Mkapa had a very high opinion of Mwalimu. He was much more politically on his line. He had come up under Mwalimu. But you can't really say that he stopped any of the privatisation. I argued with him on it, but happily because I know Ben very well. He doesn't give an inch to me either, but he would listen to Mwalimu, and he wanted to know what Mwalimu thought. He would discuss things with Mwalimu and take notes. I have no idea. Again, I was never there. If I came in, it was partly for social things, to have a cup of tea. I would stay and finish a cup of tea, and then I would leave. When Mwalimu was president, I might stay with him even afterwards. I would come in when Ben was there, and they would say, come in, we are not discussing anything secret. But you know, it is up to the president, if they had any sense, to draw on Mwalimu.

Nyerere's Regrets

JW: I can think of odd things that he regretted, but I don't think there was anything, certainly nothing major. He certainly didn't regret policies. There were other things he regretted. He regretted sending Hanga and the other two men back to Zanzibar [in 1967], where two of them were killed.[164] And nobody else was ever sent back to Zanzibar, but he regretted sending them. They were supposed to go there for questioning and then to come back. They [Hanga

---

[164] Abdullah Kassim Hanga (1932–1969) was prime minister of Zanzibar from January to April 1964. He had been Deputy General Secretary of the Afro Shiraz Party. He was executed without trial for an alleged 1967 plot to overthrow Zanzibar's president Abeid Karume. The other Zanzibari who was executed was H.E. Othman Shariff, who had been Tanzanian ambassador in Washington, D. C. from 1964 to 1965. He had also served as Minister of Education and Culture.

and Othman] never came back; one of them came back. That he regretted very much. One thing on policy, a few months before his death when he was challenged, he still said he did not regret the Arusha Declaration. If he had to rewrite it, he would only change the punctuation, but he wouldn't otherwise change it. [Laughter]

Nyerere's Accomplishments

JW: Nyerere was proud of the peace in Tanzania and the fact that the people felt that the government was on their side when he left and indeed continued to believe that he was on their side until his death. That's why it [resigning] was so dramatic for him. The fact that Tanzania stood for the independence of all developing countries, he was proud of being really non-aligned, not like Kenya that was non-aligned on one side. Tanzania was respected way beyond its size and its real importance. He was proud of the contribution we had made to the liberation of southern Africa and about the one-party system, which was more democratic in outcome than the multiparty system before the one-party system.